S0-AZE-917

H. WAYNE MORGAN is the author of several recent books on American social evolution, including *Eugene V. Debs: Socialist for President* (1962), *William McKinley and His America* (1963), and *The Gilded Age: A Reappraisal* (editor, 1963). A thoroughgoing Southwesterner, Dr. Morgan graduated from Arizona State University, took his M.A. degree at Claremont Graduate School (California), his Ph.D. at the University of California, Los Angeles, and is at present a professor of history at the University of Texas.

AMERICAN SOCIALISM

1900-1960

AMERICAN SOCIALISM

1900-1960

EDITED BY H. WAYNE MORGAN

Prentice-Hall, Inc. *Englewood Cliffs, N.J.*

Current printing (last digit):

11 10 9 8 7 6 5 4 3 2

P 03135

Contents

AMERICAN SOCIALISM

1900-1960

Introduction

MANY PEOPLE STILL REMEMBER IT, THOUGH THEY ARE GROWING RATHER gray now. They still feel a strong sense of comradeship with each other, and often exchange visits and correspond. They are almost always eager to talk about their part in the movement, "the Party" they usually call it. Despite a certain loquaciousness, they are a historian's delight. They are the old Socialists, the Americans who remember when their party and cause commanded considerable support among many segments of the American population. They have younger successors and their movement is by no means without influence, but somehow it is not the same. The oldsters recall with a kind of fervor the rallies, the picnics, reading party newspapers, home discussion circles. They remember the conventions and the confident talk of the coming Cooperative Commonwealth.

Above all, they remember with delight the sense of belonging to a vital organization. They knew that the age of competitive strife was ending in favor of humane cooperation in a society that would function honestly, smoothly, and for the greatest good of the greatest number. Why did they believe it? Because they were young before World War I, when confidence reigned, and men seemed destined to reform the evils in their life. The socialists loved the drama of common effort, the sense of purpose in working for a larger goal than self. They read confidence in the faces of their leaders and in the very air they breathed. More than one remembers how his hair stood on end when he saw hushed thousands awaiting the appearance of Eugene Debs. It was a grand moment when "Labor's Cicero" strode onstage. He waved his arms in a greeting that embraced all mankind, raising that splendid voice to the rafters and beyond on behalf of the downtrodden everywhere. The sound of his voice was infectious, as was the light in the eyes of those around him as his listeners waved their red flags and thundered their approval. Supporting him and lesser party lights by distributing pamphlets, making street corner speeches, organizing rallies and spending a little money was a small price to pay for utopia.

1

The party's golden age coincided with the Progressive Movement of the early twentieth century, but socialism came to America a generation earlier. Though it often seemed shaped by a foreign radicalism and some of its leaders spoke with accents that indicated a foreign birth, the American socialist movement owed more to its own country than to Europe. It drew on the tradition of utopian communities that flourished in the days before the Civil War, and on the whole strain of humanism, radicalism, and nonconformity in the American past. The rise of an industrial society after the Civil War, and the tensions of late nineteenth century life gave it impetus as the new century dawned.

The Socialist Labor Party, fostered after 1890 chiefly by Daniel DeLeon (1852-1914), was the first formidable socialist organization in America. DeLeon was cut on the classic pattern of socialist theorizer. Dutch and Jewish in origin, he taught international law and philosophy at Columbia University in the late 1880's. A tireless worker and patient organizer, he believed it his life's mission to spread Marxism in America. Unhappily for him, the country he chose to convert disliked theory. Though dogmatic, irascible, and narrow-minded in many of his ideas, DeLeon possessed conviction and a certain magnetism that made him the SLP's patron saint, a role he still fulfills long after his death.

DeLeon was vitally interested in labor organization and socialist agitation. Convinced that the workers directed by socialists could bring down capitalism, he attacked conservative craft labor unionists and hoped to organize a new socialist labor movement. He made many enemies and little headway. He thought that sectarian purity was the key to his kingdom and that the American workingman would welcome his doctrinal logic. He was sadly mistaken, and after 1900 his party declined into a rigid sect while the majority of American socialists went into the Socialist Party of America. In his heavy emphasis on doctrine and his fascination with the dialectical process of socialism's triumph over capitalism, "the New York pope," as enemies called him, managed to be both belligerent and dull. However important the history of his party and ideas, he stands outside the main development of American socialism.

While DeLeon purified his own thought and followers, other groups won the great majority of those inclined to socialism. By

1897 the Social Democracy of America planned to colonize a Far Western state. But the era of utopian communities was over. The Social Democracy merged by 1898 with the Social Democratic Party. The SDP, dominated by Victor L. Berger (1860-1929), believed in the promise of its own name, social democracy. Though decidedly socialist in its aim, the party taught democratic action, representative government, and a slow patient fight toward its socialist utopia. Its followers shunned revolutionary violence and talk of uprisings among the workers. Education was its key to success, and its doctrines better fitted American possibilities than did DeLeon's. Milwaukee was the laboratory of Berger's experiment. He and able lieutenants made it the most socialist city in America by shrewdly capitalizing on local needs with a socialist aim. By patient building, they created a socialist machine that was the envy of Republican and Democratic opponents. Berger was a powerful force in the socialist movement, and became a national spokesman. He was the first party member to sit in the national congress, serving as a Representative from his Milwaukee district from 1911 to 1913, and from 1923 to 1929.

The Social Democrats were builders, but they often lacked flair and color. The most famous American socialist, Eugene Victor Debs (1855-1926) brought both to the movement. A product of frontier Indiana, a youthful veteran of hard railroad life, a dynamic labor organizer, Debs combined qualities of leadership with a great love of mankind to become a formidable political campaigner and social evangelist. In 1893 he formed the American Railway Union along industrial lines. The following year he reluctantly entered the famous Pullman strike and served a jail sentence when the strike was crushed. He emerged from prison leaning toward socialism, and lent his prestige for a time to utopian comrades in the Social Democracy. By 1897 he was ready for full socialism, and rapidly became the party's chief national figure. He was a socialist candidate for president five times, served two jail sentences for his beliefs, and became one of the great figures in American radicalism.

Politics and labor agitation fascinated the socialists not merely as ways of attaining power but as means of education. The SLP had run candidates for national office in the 1890's with few results. The Social Democrats worked on the local level in the late 1890's, showing their greatest strength in Wisconsin, Massachusetts, and New York. By 1900, when Debs ran for president on a Social Democratic ticket with support from an SLP splinter group, American socialism was ripe for unity.

In 1901 the Socialist Party of America emerged from the confusion and for the rest of the century contained most of America's socialists. It was a coalition, formed of often conflicting interests, and its history revealed its nature. The SPA basically contained three groups. On the right stood Victor Berger and his step-by-step socialists, committed to education and the democratic process. In the center stood the moderates, also committed to education and the ballot, but inclined to sympathize with a stronger socialist tone in their program. On the left stood the revolutionaries, led by many rather than one man. The last group claimed Debs as their idol, but he flirted with both the moderates and conservatives. Despite his lurid oratory and biting pen, he was more often with the moderates than the radicals. The revolutionaries were militant in their desire for party recognition of radical labor unions. They frankly distrusted the "slowcialists," as they dubbed the right wing, who looked like mere reformers to men that talked of worker's revolts and social revolution.

So varied a group invited dissension, and the history of American socialism is in one measure a story of intra-party strife. Socialism involved doctrinal interpretation, attracted varied people, and fed a fervent belief in the coming utopia. Dispute was inevitable. Every socialist tended to be his own party. Because it was a coalition, the party did not enforce the rigid discipline common to European socialism. Americans, even socialists, were too strongly tinged with individualism and free speech to accept such discipline. The party's loose structure and the semi-independence of its component parts only heightened the tendency to factionalism.

The intra-party disputes at least had the merit of inviting opinion on the great issues of the day. American socialism faced most of the issues confronting old parties and in taking its stands said much of itself and its society. In the two decades before 1920 it was a vital and positive organization, waging political campaigns, running a vocal press, raising up influential and eloquent leaders. By 1912 the party had locals and newspapers in almost every state of the Union.

The movement was at the mercy of events. As it prospered its internal weaknesses magnified and its external enemies multiplied. In 1908 it mounted a spectacular national tour for Debs' presidential campaign that warned older parties of its growing strength. Between 1910 and 1912 it elected over a thousand of its members to public office across the country and had a membership over 100,000. In 1910 it elected Emil Seidel mayor of Milwaukee, and chose Victor Berger as a Representative from his home district. In 1912, Debs polled nearly 6 per cent of the national vote in the face of formidable liberals like Woodrow Wilson and Theodore Roosevelt. Socialist ideas were welcome in the homes of workers, intellectuals, and even farmers. It seemed to some conservatives and to all socialists to be the wave of the future.

But World War I and its complications ended that dream, whatever substance it might ever have had. Many socialists were pacifists and suffered official and unofficial persecution during and after the war. American reaction against the Russian revolutions of 1917 weakened the movement. In 1919 the party splintered into its component parts, ending its golden age in a welter of confusion and quarreling.

During the arid 1920's it barely clung to life, with membership plummeting, funds almost non-existent, its national leaders old or voiceless, and with few younger men to replace them. The party continued to predict capitalism's doom, and when the Great Depression blighted the early 1930's its future seemed momentarily brighter. But it was not to be. The New Deal and Second World War drained its support.

The American socialist movement is still very much alive, most generally identified in the public mind with its great national figure, Norman Thomas. But its influence is another matter. As always, its voice is louder than its numbers warrant, since it is a haven for many articulate intellectuals. It works with minority groups, maintains an interest in labor organizations, and propagandizes in a reduced program. Its aims have not changed though its means seem different. Socialism in America still posits the belief that only its principles, achieved through the democratic process, can bring order to the chaos of the twentieth century. Its humanitarian program recognizes man's need for order and emotional as well as material security; it is designed to prevent world destruction and to build more of the good life for more people.

Its future is unknown, but its past is fascinating and rewarding to the student of American history, politics, economics, and society. Its record presented in this book could easily be the starting place for a deeper and wider study of America's past and present state.

Generalizations about the Socialist Party's stand on any given issue must be approached with caution. I have tried in these readings to give a cross section of socialist thinking on the major issues the movement faced, but they should be accepted with that reservation.

Limitations of space forced me to confine myself to the main American socialist movement in the twentieth century. I have thus arbitrarily excluded the Socialist Labor Party, since I feel it lies outside the main lines of socialist development. I have not covered men, movements, and ideas identified with but not directly connected with the main movement, such as the Industrial Workers of the World, the anarchists and syndicalists, and the communists. When I speak in my editorial notes of "the party," I mean the Socialist Party of America, founded in 1901, and parent of the present Socialist Party/Social Democratic Federation.

I

Why Be a Socialist?

IN MID-TWENTIETH CENTURY, WHEN SOCIALISM HAS BEEN INCORRECTLY and unfairly tainted with the brand of communism, it is perhaps difficult to understand why Americans in rather large numbers ever accepted socialist doctrine. American socialism drew on a long heritage of dissent and social action. Before World War I it benefited from the general demand for social reform.

But this explanation is only part of the story. Complex ideas drew men and women into the socialist orbit. A sense of outrage fed the springs of radicalism in this pre-War generation. Many people suddenly realized that the American dream of self-help, initiative, and free enterprise was not enough. It had not worked quite as planned. It had produced oppressive monopolies in economics, special privilege in politics, and dangerous inequalities in society. The average progressive Democrat or Republican was simply a reformer; he wished to abolish the system's worst manifestations and retain most of both its form and content. The socialists held otherwise; for them, the system itself was wrong.

They were optimistic, holding that socialism would triumph in America in their generation. This optimism rested on three profound assumptions: (1) Capitalism was illogical as well as brutal, and therefore destined to die. Though this idea was inherent in Marx's philosophy, socialists in few other countries so ardently believed it; (2) Life was at heart unified, with all men and things sharing a common fund of humanity and interdependence. Once capitalism fell, order would return; (3) Man is not only rational but "good," that is, willing to sacrifice for others for a larger common goal than material self-interest.

Behind the façade of scientific and philosophic thought that

7

made socialism seem rational and even inevitable, lay a confidence and even a sentimentality born largely of America's own past. Socialism appealed to many because it combined logical, scientific ideas into a workable system. It also created a mysticism that gave meaning to the lives and works of many socialist thinkers and common men alike.

American socialists came from every walk of life and every part of the nation. Many were intellectuals, captivated by ideology. Others were workers, eager to employ the rapid and complete change which socialism seemed to promise. Some were farmers and minority groups, dissatisfied with capitalism's system. A deep desire to better the lot of all mankind, a basic urge to unify on human principles the chaos already emerging from the twentieth century held them together.

1

Eugene V. Debs, "How I Became a Socialist"

Though Debs' conversion to socialism was less logical than he recalled here, this selection gives an idea of the man's fervor and of the social injustice that called him to the red banner. From The Comrade, *I (April 1902), 48-49.*

. . . On the evening of February 27, 1875, the local lodge of the Brotherhood of Locomotive firemen was organized at Terre Haute, Ind., by Joshua A. Leach, then grand master, and I was admitted as a charter member and at once chosen secretary. "Old Josh Leach," as he was affectionately called, a typical locomotive fireman of his day, was the founder of the brotherhood, and I was instantly attracted by his rugged honesty, simple manner and homely speech. How well I remember feeling his large, rough hand on my shoulder, the kindly eye of an elder brother searching my own as he gently said, "My boy, you're a little young, but I believe you're in earnest and will make your mark in the brotherhood." Of course, I assured him that I would do my best. . . .

My first step was thus taken in organized labor and a new influence fired my ambition and changed the whole current of my career.

I was filled with enthusiasm and my blood fairly leaped in my veins. Day and night I worked for the brotherhood. To see its watchfires glow and observe the increase of its sturdy members were the sunshine and shower of my life. To attend the "meeting" was my supreme joy, and for ten years I was not once absent when the faithful assembled.

At the convention held in Buffalo in 1878 I was chosen associate editor of the magazine, and in 1880 I became grand secretary and treasurer. With all the fire of youth I entered upon the crusade which seemed to fairly glitter with possibilities. For eighteen hours at a stretch I was glued to my desk reeling off answers to my many correspondents. Day and night were one. Sleep was time wasted and often, when all oblivious of her presence, in the still small hours my mother's hand turned off the light, [and] I went to bed under protest. . . .

My grip was always packed; and I was darting in all directions. To tramp through a railroad yard in the rain, snow or sleet half the night, or till daybreak, to be ordered out of the roundhouse for being an "agitator," or put off a train, sometimes passenger, more often freight, while attempting to deadhead over the division, were all in the program, and served to whet the appetite of the conqueror. . . .

Through all these years I was nourished at Fountain Proletaire. I drank deeply of its waters and every particle of my tissues became saturated with the spirit of the working class. I had fired an engine and been stung by the exposure and hardship of the rail. I was with the boys in their weary watches, at the broken engine's side and often helped to bear their bruised and bleeding bodies back to wife and child again. How could I but feel the burden of their wrongs? How could the seed of agitation fail to take deep root in my heart? . . .

In 1894 the American Railway Union was organized and a braver body of men never fought the battle of the working class.

Up to this time I had heard but little of Socialism, knew practically nothing about the movement, and what little I did know was not calculated to impress me in its favor. I was bent on thorough and complete organization of the railroad men and ultimately the whole working class, and all my time and energy were given to that end. My supreme conviction was that if they were only organized in every branch of service and all acted together in concert they could redress their wrongs and regulate the conditions of their employment. The stockholders of the corporation acted as one, why not the men? It was such a plain proposition—simply to follow the example set before their eyes by their masters—surely they could not fail to see it, act as one, and solve the problem.

It is useless to say that I had yet to learn the workings of the capitalist system, the resources of its masters, and the weakness of its slaves. Indeed, no shadow of a "system" fell athwart my pathway; no thought of ending wage-misery marred my plans. I was too deeply absorbed in perfecting wage-servitude and making it a "thing of beauty and a joy forever."

It all seems strange to me now, taking a backward look, that my vision so focalized on a single objective point that I utterly failed to see what now appears as clear as the noonday sun—so clear that I marvel that any workingman, however dull, uncomprehending, can resist it. . . .

Next followed the final shock—the Pullman strike—and the American Railway Union again won, clear and complete. The combined corporations were paralyzed and helpless. At this juncture there was delivered, from wholly unexpected quarters, a swift succession of blows that blinded me for an instant and then opened wide my eyes—and in the gleam of every bayonet and the flash of every rifle the class struggle was revealed. This was my first lesson in Socialism, though wholly unaware that it was called by that name.

An army of detectives, thugs, and murderers was equipped with badge and beer and bludgeon and turned loose; old hulks of cars were fired; the alarm bells tolled; the people were terrified; the most startling rumors were set afloat . . . injunctions flew thick and fast, arrests followed, and our office and headquarters, heart of the strike, was sacked, torn out, and nailed up by the "lawful" authorities of the federal government; and when in company with my loyal comrades I found myself in Cook County Jail at Chicago with the whole press screaming conspiracy, treason, and murder, . . . I had another exceedingly practical and impressive lesson in Socialism. . . .

The Chicago jail sentences were followed by six months at Woodstock and it was here that Socialism gradually laid hold of me in its own irresistible fashion. Books and pamphlets and letters from Socialists came by every mail and I began to read and think and dissect the anatomy of the system in which workingmen, however organized, could be shattered and battered and splintered at a single stroke. The writings of Bellamy and Blatchford early appealed to me. The "Cooperative Commonwealth" of Gronlund also impressed me, but the writings of Kautsky were so clear and conclusive that I readily grasped, not merely his argument, but also caught the spirit of his Socialist utterance—and I thank him and all who helped me out of darkness into light.

It was at this time, when the first glimmerings of Socialism were beginning to penetrate, that Victor L. Berger—and I have loved him ever since—came to Woodstock, as if a providential instrument, and delivered the first impassioned message of Socialism I had ever heard—the very first to set the "wires humming in my system." As a souvenir of that visit there is in my library a volume of "Capital," by Karl Marx, inscribed with the compliments of Victor L. Berger, which I cherish as a token of priceless value.

The American Railway Union was defeated but not conquered—overwhelmed but not destroyed. It lives and pulsates in the Socialist movement, and its defeat but blazed the way to economic freedom and hastened the dawn of human brotherhood.

2

Frederic F. Heath, "How I Became a Socialist"

A prominent party writer and lecturer, Heath started life as a Blaine Republican, then went left, and finally settled in socialism's center as a social democrat. His right-left-center pilgrimage is typical of many socialists. From The Comrade, *II (April 1903), 154-155.*

. . . I supposed I was a Republican because that political faith represented my philosophy of life. That party had given black slavery its quietus, and I had imbibed strong anti-slavery ideas from my maternal grandsire, whose tall, spare frame actually shook at the mere thought of a "copperhead." And then did not the Republican party stand for "protection" to American labor? And was I not an apprentice and "protected" to the extent of my $2 a week salary! Most certainly I was. Such arguments as I used to have!

Two years later I was ekeing out a beggarly weekly income in Chicago at my trade (drawing on wood) and not lucky enough to get steady employment. . . . I will never forget with what feelings of concern we heard one evening the sound of a nearby explosion. It was the detonation of the Haymarket bomb! The days that followed were full of excitement, which the newspapers, with an eye to business, did their best to keep alive. Then the trial came on and I gloried in the travesty on justice that followed, and looked as leniently on the packing of the jury that was to avenge "law and order," as I had on the tatoo marks on the epidermis of Blaine's political career. My benchmates were divided in sentiment. But I had heard enough and read enough to know, deep down in my inner consciousness, that the Haymarket tragedy was not part of a conscious plan to enforce restitution to the plundered myriads of toil, but rather the culmination of a series of clashes between an assortment of social rebels speaking a foreign tongue, and a notoriety-loving police cabal, egged on by the capitalist press for both mercenary and class reasons. This was a conviction that I smothered for the time. But the Haymarket bomb had its message for me, nevertheless. It forced my attention to conditions I had previously, as a dutiful Republican, failed to see.

Yet in spite of the influence of surroundings, I believe I was always a democrat. I always had a hatred of caste, and of artificial superiorities. As a member of the work-a-day army I was painfully conscious of the vulgarity and unwholesomeness of the whole fabric of toil and of toil's *dramatis personae*. In time I grew into the stoutest kind of rebel. I evolved a philosophy of my own. I became impatient that the lower classes did not partake of the culture and the refinements that minister to a satisfactory life, and came in time to blame conditions and not the workers for it. I grew to be reflective. I remember that I noted the fact that the first ambition of the Negro who drifted north was to make a good appearance and dress well, even though this latter was often carried to the lengths of caricature. I saw that there was in the breasts of all persons, white or black, the desire for self-betterment, no matter how little the possibility of attaining their ideal. . . .

There was one criticism that Socialism made as to the capitalist system that I was in a position to understand. That was the utterly reckless and planless way in which capitalism ruled in the industrial field. I had at different periods of my life been a printer, a wood engraver, and an artist for wood engravers. I had practically given my time to my employers as an apprentice for the sake of learning trades that were later rendered practically useless by the developments of industry. . . . And it was not hard to see that the same sort of fate was overtaking other workers and forcing them to readjust themselves, as best they could, in the work-army.

. . . My introduction to the actual Socialist movement was due to three influences. First, there was the paper that J. A. Wayland used to print at Greensburg, Indiana, . . . Then there were stray copies of Socialist Labor Party literature that came my way. And, finally, I struck up an acquaintance with Victor L. Berger. . . . The Milwaukee Socialist movement at that time was a large one, wholly outside the S.L.P. (which was regarded as too narrow and stagnating), and was composed of German-Americans. The word got abroad among them that a Yankee had turned Socialist, and they began to see the beginning of the end! The great desire among the German Socialists in the country at that time was to have Socialism become native to the soil; for they saw that there could be no progress otherwise. . . . I attended a meeting of their club without understanding a word that was said, and was urged to work toward the establishment of an English-speaking branch, some of them agreeing to join. At this time, like the typical convert, the intensity of my Socialism was unbounded. I was terribly academic. I had the S.L.P. habit, strongly developed. Ordinary words were too tame; phrases were my "long suite," and I remember now, when we were about to form the English-speaking branch at last, it was my suggestion that the fact of having read Marx's "Capital" should be the badge of eligibility to membership! Luckily this proposition was not agreed to, and so the club grew in membership and influence—and Marx escaped again being made a fetish. . . .

The years that have followed have mellowed my conception of Socialism, luckily. The Socialism presented by the Socialist Labor

Party soon grew to be repugnant to me. I could not square it with my love of democracy. I came to realize that a Co-operative Commonwealth secured through a cataclysm was a wild dream indeed, and not at all in accordance with the teachings of history. And I felt also that if Socialism was to be a condition of society in which autocratic or bureaucratic rule was to exist I should in all probability be in rebellion against it. I wanted my Socialism to be democratically administered; I wanted the whole people to rule. . . .

. . . Socialism in American today [1903] is virile and all-conquering just because it has ceased to be cataclysmic, and therefore utopian. It is a proposition that is simply unanswerable, and loses nothing by being stated in simple language. We live in a most favored time. I thank my stars that it has been given to me to live just at this particular stage in the world's history, when there is such a wonderful cause to be won. I can think of nothing more inspiring, unless it be Social Democracy realized.

3

Morris Hillquit, "Has It Been Worthwhile?"

A moderate socialist, originally a DeLeon follower, Hillquit was the movement's shrewdest compromiser and a brilliant legal talent. In his twilight years he reminisced on what socialism had meant to him, in a vein typical of almost all old party members. From Loose Leaves From a Busy Life *(New York: The Macmillan Company, 1934), pp. 321-332. By permission of Mrs. Sylvia Angrist.*

. . . To me Socialism has never been a mere abstract philosophy or intellectual pastime. It has been my ideal and religion and one of my principal interests in life. I have given my whole adult existence to the service of the cause.

Has it been worthwhile?

I would not be candid if I did not confess that in the periods of heavy defeats I had moments of disappointment and discouragement, black moments of doubt and misgiving, when I asked myself the tantalizing question.

I always emerged from the soul-searching quest with an abiding conviction that my course was right and that my work was not in vain. . . . I utterly reject the opinion that the Socialist movement has been a failure. What is failure, what is success in the struggle for a high humanitarian cause, or for that matter, in the life of the individual?

I have never considered Socialism as purely or even mainly a political movement. Socialism is above all a philosophy of life and civilization. It aims at a saner, higher, and nobler social order. Its concrete task is to prepare and to develop the economic, intellectual, and moral foundations of a better world to come. The progress of such a movement cannot be measured by any concrete tests. It can hardly be measured at all. Who can be so bold as to say that the Socialist propaganda has not left a deep imprint on American thought and mind?

Forty years ago the theory and policy of our government was rampantly individualistic. The dominant article of the American political creed was the principle of noninterference with the struggles of the rich and the poor, the strong and the weak. The government kept studiously aloof from the assumption of economic or social functions. Today the principle of individualism in government is largely an outworn political fiction. . . . The spirit of Socialism, which places the welfare of society above the selfish interests of the individual, clearly characterizes the whole modern trend of American governmental policy, and much of it is directly traceable to the work of Socialist propaganda.

It is interesting to note how many reforms first formulated as political planks by the Socialists have been enacted into law by the old parties under pressure of economic necessity and public clamor.

The Socialist vote and party membership are no index to the extent to which Socialistic thought has permeated the population of the country. . . .

It is a mistake to assume that because the Socialist movement in the United States has made no appreciable and visible progress in the last forty years it may not prove victorious in the course of the next twenty years, and it is equally false to infer that when the movement resumes its growth, it will necessarily be regular and gradual, and that it may not proceed by leaps and bounds.

I am hopeful of seeing a great and powerful, perhaps even a triumphant Socialist movement in this country in my own days.

But whether I live to see the realization of the Socialist goal or not is after all not a matter of prime importance.

There is, strictly speaking, no such thing as a final social goal. The social horizon, like the physical horizon, is only an illusory line marking our visual limitation.

To the person who does not move from the spot it remains at a stationary and fixed distance. To the traveller who proceeds on his onward path it is a shifting and unattainable goal. As he advances toward the horizon, it recedes from him, uncovering ever new stretches ahead of him, unfolding ever new vistas before his eyes. . . .

To me the Socialist movement with its enthusiasm and idealism, its comradeship and struggles, its hopes and disappointments, its victories and defeats, has been the best that life has had to offer.

4

Oscar Ameringer, "If You Don't Weaken"

A German immigrant endowed with musical abilities as well as social aims, Ameringer was a socialist organizer and propagandizer in the Indian Territory in frontier days, and later a leading radical newsman in Oklahoma. His recollections show clearly the outrage that motivated many people to join the socialist crusade. From If You Don't Weaken *(New York: Holt, Rinehart and Winston, Inc. 1940), pp. 232-233. By permission of Mrs. Oscar Ameringer.*

. . . I am not exaggerating [in recounting a trip through Oklahoma's backlands]. As the days grew into weeks, I found worse. . . . I found toothless old women with sucking infants on their withered breasts. I found a hospitable old hostess, around thirty or less, her hands covered with rags and exzema, offering me a biscuit with those hands, apologizing that her biscuits were not as good as she used to make because with her sore hand she could no longer knead the dough as it ought to be. I saw youngsters emaciated by hookworms, malnutrition, and pellagra, who had lost their second teeth before they were twenty years old. I saw tottering old male wrecks with the infants of their fourteen-year-old wives on their laps. . . . I saw humanity at its lowest possible level of degradation and decay. I saw smug, well-dressed, overly-fed hypocrites march to church on Sabbath day, Bibles under their arms, praying for God's kingdom on earth while fattening like latter-day cannibals on the share-croppers. I saw wind-jamming, hot-air-spouting politicians geysering Jeffersonian platitudes about equal rights to all and special privileges to none; about all men born equal with the rights to life, liberty, and the pursuit of happiness without even knowing, much less caring, that they were addressing as wretched a set of abject slaves as ever walked the face of the earth, anywhere or at any time. The things I saw on that trip are the things you never forget.

What those people needed, what they need today, is not pious soothing syrup and political Castoria. What they needed was not uplift from above, no matter how well meant, but upheaval from below that would give them a big and good enough share of God's footstool on which to work, rear their children, and restore to themselves the dignity of human beings. Goethe says youth is revolutionary, maturity conservative, old age reactionary. Well, I am nearing seventy, but I still regard a social arrangement in which some possess thousands of acres of life-giving earth, while millions of children are born without enough to plant their little pink bottoms on, a black betrayal of democracy, an insult to Christianity. . . .

5

Rev. G. E. Littlefield, "Why I Shall Vote the Socialist Ticket"

This selection shows the blend of optimism, rationality, and confidence so common to socialist thinking. From The Arena, *XXXII (October 1904), 397-398.*

. . . First: Socialism means economic security to every worker; substituting cooperation and equal opportunity for competition and class-privilege. . . .

Second: Socialism will prolong human life and make it happier. . . . When the People is its own capitalist, the treadmill of toil and the worry of loss will be eliminated, so that the average life will be nearer the Psalmist's three-score-and-ten, and happier on account of all these reasons.

Third: Socialism will foster nobler incentives. . . .

Fourth: Socialism will help evolve a higher individualism. . . .

Fifth: Socialism will advance morality. . . . Socialism will cease plastering and patching a rotten system and substitute justice for injustice, placing the premium upon the Golden Rule instead of on the anarchy of "every one for himself and the devil take the hindmost."

Sixth: Socialism will make religion real. . . .

Seventh: Socialism will secure the home, save women from shame, and stop the sacrifice of children to the Moloch of commercialism.

Eighth: Socialism will make for temperance. The saloon will go out of business when the incentive of profit is removed, and men will less crave stimulants when we have more wholesome conditions of life.

Ninth: Socialism will purify politics and perfect true democracy. . . . Government of the rich, by the rich, for the rich will be replaced by government of the people, by the people, and for the people.

Tenth: Socialism will abolish war. International comrades in a world-wide Cooperative Commonwealth will not kill one another.

Eleventh: Socialism will settle the labor question and thus avert another possible civil war. Industrial partners will not strike against themselves.

Twelfth: I am a Socialist because Socialism is inevitable. Capitalism and wageism, like two cobras, will crush each other. . . . Either this, or else the world goes back into the melting-pot through another dark age of despotism.

6

Covington Hall, "Why I Am A Socialist"

Though a triumph of bad poetry, the following selection well illustrates the naïveté and sentimentality, as well as the honest humanism that motivated many socialists. From The International Socialist Review, *V (December 1904).*

I have heard the child-slaves weeping when the world was fair
    and bright,
Heard them begging, begging, begging for the playgrounds and
    the light!
I have seen the "statesmen" holding all save truth a vested right,
And the priest and preacher fighting in the legions of the Night.

I have seen the queens of fashion in their jewelled pride arrayed,
Ruby crowned and splendid,—rubies of a baby's life blood made,
Richer than the gems of nature, of a stranger, deeper shade,
On their snow white bosoms quivered as the dames of fashion
    prayed.

Then I looked into the dungeons where the brute-men cringe and
    crawl—
Men to every high thought blinded—men who were not men at
    all—
And my eyes glanced upward to the men whom we "successful"
    call,
And the Beast was in their foreheads and their thrones about to
    fall.

And I've seen my father lying on his death-bed like a beast,
In his poverty forsaken, he a Southern soldier priest;
Seen his broken body tremble as the pulse of living ceased,
And his soul go outward, moaning, as the red sun lit the east.

And I've seen my little mother on her death-bed weep and moan
For the babies she was leaving in the great world all alone;
Heard her loving spirit, seeking something to atone—
How she feared the god of hunger! How she feared the heart of
    stone!

And you talk to me "religion," and "rebellion" you "deplore,"
You whose souls have never anguished at the death watch of
    the poor!
You who rape the starving millions and yet grasp for more and
    more,
Can you blame us if we curse you as the beggar's crumbs you
    throw?

In these wild and frightful moments I have felt my reason reel,
Felt an impulse like the tiger's over all my person steal;
Felt it would not be a murder if my hand the blow could deal,
That would brand upon your temple the death angel's mark and
    seal.

Then I heard a voice crying, "Workers of the world, unite!"
And the vanguard of the Marxians broke upon my hopeless sight.
High above them, proudly waving, streamed the blood-red flag
    of Right,
As they faced the hosts of Darkness and the high priests of the
    Night.

Thoughts of murder vanished from me and the anarch ceased to
    reign,
For the scheme of life unravelled and, at last, God's work seemed
    sane.
And I took my place beside them, there upon Truth's battle
    plain—
And I stand beside them fighting till the world we lose or gain.

II

Socialism and the Existing Order

IN A COUNTRY BLESSED WITH MATERIAL ABUNDANCE AND THE HOPE OF easy prosperity, not often given to personal sacrifice, how could socialism gain headway? To attack capitalism, private enterprise, and materialism in a nation that had profited so much from all three took courage and logic, as well as a flair for the dramatic.

By "Capitalism" the socialists meant the total social system that flowed, in their view, from an economy privately administered for personal profit. In simple, classic Marxian fashion they argued that wealth belonged to its creators—the workers. The economy of a nation determined its politics, society, and culture; when capitalism dissolved in favor of the new cooperative order, all spheres of life would improve. The socialists were willing to dispose of capitalism gradually. They realized how large the task would be, and hoped that once a dramatic start was made, the system would fall of its own weight. As private ownership and materialism lessened, they argued, people would think in terms of the total good. The Cooperative Commonwealth would emerge triumphantly and logically from capitalism.

The socialists wished to nationalize the nation's basic industries, but confiscation was never an official party policy. Debs, some labor leaders, and a few radical socialists might hint otherwise, but the party relied on representative democracy to dispense with the old order. The socialists were not trust busters. Trusts were merely a logical outcome of history. Once put in the people's hands and run for the good of all they would pose no problem.

It was not difficult for the socialists to attract sympathy by attacking the evils of capitalism and the existing social order. These were much more evident at the turn of the century than now. The gulf

21

between the Haves and the Have-nots was the chief topic of conversation in the decade before World War I. Class lines were more clearly drawn. The distance between the comfortable and the poor in that era was a stark reality of daily life for millions. The socialist proposal to close it rapidly made sense to many.

The slogans surrounding capitalism did not attract the socialists. There was scant individualism in an economy dominated by trusts, they argued. They pointed out that in a world grown interdependent, there was no individualism but that attained by working with others and for the total social good. The profit motive, capitalism's most vaunted shibboleth, had produced a grasping social ethic, a modified law of the jungle; slums as well as palaces, low wages and high dividends, a working class and an idle class. A new spirit of cooperation, a different kind of self-help, was not only logical but inevitable to socialists.

But the socialists knew America, and frustrating as the battle was, they also knew how formidable were the institutions they attacked. They proposed, therefore, a compromise assault on the existing order. They would not abolish private property altogether. They were more concerned with oppressive monopoly that affected the total good than with private property as such. Standard Oil might be nationalized under their program, but not necessarily the corner grocery. Behind this compromise on the question of private ownership, which did not differ markedly from most European social democracy, lay the deep belief in the common goals to be attained by common labor. Much of socialism's propaganda seems unreal without understanding the confident milieu in which it functioned before World War I. It offered to take from the few and give to the many; to replace political inequality with democratic government and civil liberties; to revamp society on the equality that had buttressed the American Dream and which had not as yet come to life.

1

"The New God": Socialism and Conspiracy

The socialists saw society in black-white terms; the Few oppressed the Many. The following poem well expresses the simple logic that flowed from such a proposition. From The Appeal to Reason, *May 3, 1902.*

I came to a mill by the river side,
'Twas half a mile long and nearly as wide,
With blazing fires and an army of men,
Toiling at furnace, shovel and pen.
What a most magnificent plant! I cried,
When a workman in overalls replied:

Chorus:
It's Morgan's, it's Morgan's the great financial gorgon.
Everything here but the atmosphere all belongs to Morgan.

I dwelt in a nation filled with pride;
Her people were many, her lands were wide;
Her record in war, in science and art,
Proved she'd the brains, the muscle and the heart.
America's a grand old country, I cried,
When a man who was out on strike replied:

Chorus:
Every railroad train, every ship on the main, all belongs to
    Morgan.

I went to Heaven. The jasper walls
Were high and wide, and the golden halls
Shone bright beyond; but a strange new mark
Was over the gate. It read, "Private Park."
Why, what's the meaning of this, I cried,
When a saint with a harp in his hands replied:

Chorus:
If you want cheap rates to the Heavenly gate you'll have to
    apply to Morgan.

I went to the only place left for me,
So I boarded the boat for the brimstone sea.
Maybe I'll be allowed to sit
On the griddled floor of the bottomless pit.
But a jeering imp with horns on his face,
Cried out as he forked me out of the place:

Chorus:
Get off that spot; we're keeping it hot; that seat is reserved for
Morgan.

2

"The Ferment": Socialist Hopes for Success

*In the years before 1914, the socialists saw every reason to hope
for success within a generation. Their unbounded enthusiasm re-
flected the belief in immediate gains, as the following editorial
shows. From* The Appeal to Reason, *May 3, 1902.*

The conditions everywhere, in everything, seem to be in a ferment such as was never before known. In religious, in industrial, in
political affairs strife and discord seem to be holding high carnival.
At the bottom of it all is the industrial [problem]—from it
spring all the ills that beset the religious and political fields. Combines are monopolizing the food and other necessities of the people,
strikes are resulting in thousands of industries and the people are
looking about them as never before to see what the world-wide com-
motion means. Petty wars are being waged by strong nations against
weaker ones, to force them to buy goods for the profit of the master
class in the strong countries, and inside the strong countries
threatened revolution is hovering like a nightmare over the rule of
the classes. The laboring people for the first time in the world's history, are taking an interest in the social and industrial conditions,
and are feeling the power which a better understanding has given
them. In Europe they are questioning the rights of the ruler to continue the Old Order. They are meeting in the halls of legislation
and measuring mental forces with them to the discomfiture of the
masters. A great change is taking place; every day is different from

yesterday; tomorrow will be still different; the whole world of thought is moving to new bases; old ideas are thrown away and new ones are rapidly replacing them; labor is receiving new inspirations and new hopes; it is marching from one vantage to another. The changes that have occurred in two years might almost be said to have created a new world of action, so great has it been. The changed conditions almost daze the observer. The portending changes [are] different from any that [have] ever been attempted; other changes [were] simply replacing one ruler by another; one religion by another. This [new change] means the laboring people propose to be masters of the earth, and they will brook no other masters. They are everywhere questioning the right of the masters to say how long they shall labor, what they shall receive or what they shall pay for what they buy. They are virtually denying the right of private capital—for they are denying the right of the possessor to have absolute control. The master class, like its prototype barons of old, will contest every inch and will thus cause labor to make a harder struggle, to go further than it would without this opposition. Labor will advance from one position to another until its demand will be for the abolition of private capital. It does not know it today, but that is where it must logically arrive. The next ten years will be the most momentous in the history of the race, judged by the present ferment.

3

Morris Hillquit, "Socialism and Individualism"

As the movement gained ground, the socialists clarified their stand on individualism. Their general position was best stated formally in Hillquit's writings. From Socialism in Theory and Practice *(New York: The Macmillan Company, 1909), pp. 26-29. By permission of Mrs. Sylvia Angrist.*

. . . Let us take the most simple articles of use: the coat we wear, the chair we sit on, the bed we sleep in, and ask ourselves, Who produced these articles? To answer that question we shall have to consider the unknown thousands who contributed to the work of their immediate design and manufacture, to the production and transportation of the material contained in them, to the work of constructing the wonderful machinery employed at the countless steps of process, and to the work of operating the machinery of transportation, etc. In modern production the individual laborer is practically obliterated; what is before us is a world-wide community of socially organized labor of all gradations, from the highest and most skillful to the lowest and most common, working together collectively for the needs of our race.

And it is this collective labor of our time that sustains modern comforts and modern civilization. Were it possible for us to return to the regime of absolute individualism in production, to prepare our own food, make our own clothing, build our own dwellings, without taking advantage of the material prepared by others, without accepting the cooperation of our fellow men, we should relapse into a state of savagery in less than a generation.

While the feature of individualism has been almost eliminated from the field of production by the last century, it has, during that period, showed much greater vitality in the sphere of management of our industries.

The management of our industries by individualists for their own private benefit and in rivalry with each other—*industrial competition*—has for decades been the favorite topic of controversy between the adherents of the individualist philosophy and the partisans of the socialist school of political economy. To the sturdy individualist the competitive system of industry is the source of all blessings of civilization: he never tires of extolling the merits of that system as an incentive to industrial enterprise, inventiveness and efficiency, as a character builder and lever of all social and individual progress. The socialist, on the other hand, points a warning finger to the evils of competition: the anarchy in management and waste in production which the system entails, and the tremendous social, economic, and ethical losses which it imposes on the producers, the consumers and the community at large.

But while the discussion on the merits and demerits of competition is assuming ever more intense forms, the mute forces of economic revolution, unconcerned by theories and abstractions, are rapidly working toward a practical solution of the problem. The individual capitalist steadily yields his place in the industrial world to the corporation and the trust, and the latter combine and consolidate the independent managements of numerous individual concerns under one corporate direction, and reorganize the management of industries, frequently on a national and even international scale. The irresistible growth of trusts and monopolies is the central fact of all recent economic development, and it sounds the death knell of individual competition.

The only sphere of our industrial life in which the principle of individualism has survived in all its pristine vigor, is that of the appropriation or distribution of the products.

Although the instruments of production have become social in their character and use, and indispensable to the entire working community, they are still owned and controlled by the individual capitalists. Although the production of goods is a collective process, and its management and direction are fast becoming so, it is still conducted principally for the benefit of the individual captains of industry. Although all useful members of the community collectively contribute to the so-called national wealth, only a comparatively small number of individuals share in it. In short, although the production of wealth is practically socialistic, its distribution is entirely individualistic.

And this contradiction between the modern methods of production and distribution is the only real issue between the individualist and the socialist in the domain of economic discussion.

The beneficiaries of the present system of wealth distribution have a very obvious material interest in maintaining it, and there never was a ruling class that did not have the abundant support of scientific and ethical theories to justify it in the continued enjoyment of its privileges. In the present case this function is being performed by the school of "individualistic" philosophers and moralizers.

The socialists, on the other hand, consider the present system of individual appropriation of social wealth as an anachronism, a survival of a past economic order, and a disturbing factor in the process of social, economic and ethical progress.

The main object of socialism is to adjust the principles of wealth distribution to those of production—to make the one as social and general in function and effect as the other already is. . . .

4

A. W. Ricker, "The Most Frequent Objections to Socialism Answered"

In less academic tone and with more color and immediacy than Hillquit's writing, the party's pamphleteers explained why socialism was practical, what it would mean to individualism, and why it should be adopted. From The Socialist Congressional Campaign Book, 1914 *(Chicago: The Socialist Party, 1914), pp. 12-15.*

THAT SOCIALISTS WANT TO DIVIDE UP

Do you mean by this a division of the farms, houses, money, and wealth of the country? This would not only be impossible but foolish. We do not stand for a division of property but for PUBLIC OWNERSHIP of certain kinds of property. We now publicly own the streets, highways, schools, post office system, and in some places the electric light and water systems. . . . We could not divide what is called the machinery of production and distribution, such as the shops, factories, mines, and railroads. These industries are not owned by private individuals now, but by cooperative associations of capitalists called "trusts." The Socialists propose to transfer the title of property now owned by the trusts to the people of the United States. The only thing we have ever thought of dividing is the opportunity to work in the great public enterprises which, under Socialism, will be open to both men and women. In other words, we propose to divide the jobs.

THAT SOCIALISM WILL DO AWAY
WITH PRIVATE PROPERTY

On the contrary, Socialism will make it easier to get private property. The workers have very little private property. . . . The capitalists ultimately get the wealth created by labor. When the ownership of industries on which profits are filched from labor passes to the people then the useful workers will get, not only what they now receive, but also that part of their earnings which go to the capitalist as profit. It will then be possible for the working people to own their own homes and such other property as ought to belong to individuals.

THAT SOCIALISM IS AGAINST RELIGION

Socialism is an economic and not a religious question. What a man believes or does not believe about religion does not enter into the solution of the bread and butter question. The capitalist class exploits and robs the working class regardless of what the latter believe about religion, or what is their color, race, or sex. Since the capitalists exploit all of us in common, regardless of whether we are Catholic or Protestant, black or white, male or female, we therefore ought to stand up solidly together as a united working class fighting for one common end—our own industrial freedom. . . .

THAT SOCIALISM WILL REDUCE EVERYONE
TO A DEAD LEVEL

On the contrary, it is capitalism that is reducing the socially useful class to a dead level—the level of the cheapest wage for which the workers may be had. . . . If Socialism does establish a level, that level will certainly be a higher one than is now possible for 80 per cent of the population.

THAT WE CAN'T GET POSSESSION OF THE MACHINERY
OF PRODUCTION AND DISTRIBUTION NOW HELD
BY THE CAPITALIST CLASS

Sure, we can. And by perfectly legal and constitutional methods, too. Some we can buy. Some we can build ourselves. Some we can get by foreclosure. Some by making provision for public ownership in the franchises, and some we can get by exercising the right of eminent domain.

THAT YOU CAN'T CHANGE HUMAN NATURE

Then you ought to quit preaching to people to be Christlike. You can change humanity just as you can change the small wild peach to the big juicy tame one, the sour crab apple to the big red apple of the orchard, the little speckled ear of corn of the Indian to the big yellow one of the modern cornfield. Human nature has changed from savagery to barbarism, then to civilization. It will change to Socialism, and come to measurable perfection just like the sour crab apple became, under proper environment, a big mellow pippin. . . .

THAT SOCIALISM WILL DESTROY PERSONAL LIBERTY AND FORCE PEOPLE TO DO WHAT THEY DON'T WANT TO DO

Mistaken again. Socialism will increase personal liberty for those who have but little now. None of us do exactly as we want to do, not even the rich. Do people want to work in sweat shops; do children want to work in factories in the playtime of life; do women like to wash for a living; does anybody like to clean spitoons; do sheriffs like to evict people from their homes; do judges like to send people to jail; do women like to become prostitutes; does anyone love to hoe cotton in the burning sun? You see we do things because it is necessary to do them more often than because we like to. There will be many unpleasant tasks under Socialism. We will perform them with machinery so far as possible. Our hours will be shorter and our work pleasanter and safer, but we will still do some things we don't want to do.

THAT SOCIALISM WON'T WORK

My dear skeptic, you have said that about every piece of machinery invented. You said of the first railroad that the noise of the engine would dry up the cows and scare the chickens out of the summer crop of eggs. Of the first steamboat, that the boiler would blow up and the ship couldn't carry enough coal to make a trip across the sea. . . . How you laughed at the first automobile. You don't laugh at these things any more. They are machines which DO work, but most of them are made to work YOU. All are used in such a way as to harvest a bigger crop for the trusts to divide. Now Socialism is an economic machine through which system the people will own the whole process of production and distribution. Those who understand it know it will work. Those who laugh at it are just like those who laughed at the binder and the cream separator.

WE CAN'T GET ALONG WITHOUT A BOSS

About half the people at the time of the revolution said we couldn't get along without a king, but we have. Under Socialism we will have a manager, of course, of each industry. Let's call this manager the boss for convenience. NOW the boss works for the capitalist. Under Socialism he will work for YOU. NOW he figures to make more profits, for his owner, out of your hides. Under Socialism he will study to make hours shorter and work safer and saner. You will elect him and if he isn't satisfactory you will fire him and get another. . . .

III

Socialism and Labor

THE WORKER, WHETHER ALREADY ORGANIZED IN A LABOR UNION OR still drifting, was socialism's most immediate target. He was the source of strength for most European socialist parties. He was presumably dissatisfied with his status in the capitalist system, and stood to gain much from socialism's proposed reforms. The conservative labor unions typified by the railroad brotherhoods and the American Federation of Labor had done nothing dramatic to change his status; nor had they organized large numbers of American workers. To the socialists, the craft unions were merely a phase of capitalism, since they cooperated with the "master class" and would reform the existing order merely to increase some workers' immediate material state.

Many socialists, like Debs, came from the American labor movement. Some of the more radical unions, like the Western Federation of Miners, and the Industrial Workers of the World, bore a distinct socialist tinge. Both Debs and DeLeon helped found the IWW. DeLeon was quickly expelled for doctrinal differences, and Debs left the organization because he disliked its incoherent radicalism and suspicious leanings toward syndicalism. But he always defended the IWW's effort to defeat craft unionism's hold on the American worker.

DeLeon's technique of "dual unionism," a frontal assault on the A.F. of L. by establishing a rival union, the Socialist Trade and Labor Alliance, failed. Its most salient effect was to arouse suspicion of all things radical and socialistic among conservative labor leaders of Samuel Gompers' generation. Most socialists within the party after 1900 advocated the technique of "boring from within." If an

assault from outside was too much for their resources, they could attack from within and hope to capture and revolutionize existing
labor unions.

Few issues so divided the socialist movement as the party's attitude
toward organized labor. It cut to the heart of what kind of socialism would come to America. The left wing socialists wanted un-
ceasing radical propaganda, official recognition of the IWW after
1905, and open assault on the craft unions and their leaders. The
"slowcialists" urged caution, realizing that a fight with organized
labor could affect socialism's appeal all along the line. Energy spent
on this fight, from their view, could be better spent elsewhere.

But whatever their differences over techniques and attitudes toward labor, socialists agreed on the purpose of their work. If they
captured labor's votes they could either win dramatic election victories, adding momentum to the cause, or become a potent third
force to hold the balance between the two older parties. He who
controlled the economy controlled the society. Organized labor was
basic to their whole program.

Their hard work, often shaded with divisive bitterness, brought
small reward. Indoctrinating the American worker with socialism
was like pushing an elephant uphill. It required both dazzling
propaganda and patience. The socialists never dominated a major
labor union, though they had support in the A.F. of L. until
World War I and were powerful in brewing and garment unions.
How many workers voted for Debs is unknown, but because of his
own labor background and magnetic appeal, he won the official
support of some small unions and must have carried many more
silent workers with him.

Socialism's gains within the labor movement were temporary,
and the socialists lacked the strength to support a labor movement
of their own. They could not wean the American worker from the
ideals or myths that had so captivated his society. He usually
thought free enterprise just as feasible for him as for the entrepre-
neur. He prized materialism and wanted more pay and shorter
hours, goals whose immediacy he could understand, rather than a
distant utopia. The socialists could not defeat his affinity for reform
within the existing system, or his belief that there were no rigid

classes in America. They could not transmit to the worker their own belief in cooperative work and disbelief in the free enterprise system.

1

"The Socialist Platform and Labor Organization"

The following plank from the party's platform of 1912 shows the forces at work for compromise in wording socialism's official attitude toward unions. On the one hand, labor should join for common socialist cause; on the other, the party does not suggest violence against existing unions. From The Proceedings of the National Convention of the Socialist Party, 1912 (*Chicago: The Socialist Party, 1912*), *p. 195.*

ADOPTED BY THE CONVENTION:

Political organization and economic organization are alike necessary in the struggle for working class emancipation. The most harmonious relations ought to exist between the two great forces of the working class movement—the Socialist Party and the Labor Unions.

The labor movement of the United States has of recent years made marvellous progress in all directions. It has steadily increased in numbers and has reached trades and industries which were before unorganized. It has in many instances concentrated its power and increased its efficiency by the amalgamation of related trades into federations and industrial unions. Many unions have opened their meetings and journals to the discussion of vital social and political problems of the working class and have repudiated the demoralizing politics represented by the National Civic Federation. The organized workers are rapidly developing an enlightened and militant class-consciousness.

The reality of this progress is attested by the increasing virulence with which the organized capitalists wage their war against the union. This improved economic organization is not a matter of abstract theory, but grows out of the experience of the wage workers in the daily class struggle. Only those actually engaged in the struggle in the various trades and industries can solve the problems of form and organization.

The Socialist Party therefore reaffirms the position it has always taken with regard to the movement of organized labor:

a. That the party has neither the right nor the desire to interfere in any controversies which may exist within the labor union movement over questions of form of organization or technical methods of action in the industrial struggle, but trusts to the labor organizations themselves to solve these questions.

b. That the Socialists call the attention of their brothers in the labor unions to the vital importance of the task of organizing the unorganized, especially the immigrants and the unskilled laborers, who stand in greatest need of organized protection and who will constitute a great menace to the progress and welfare of organized labor if they remain neglected. The Socialist Party will ever be ready to co-operate with the labor unions in the task of organizing the unorganized workers, and urges all labor organizations, who have not already done so, to throw their doors wide open to the workers of their respective trades and industries, abolishing all onerous conditions of membership and artificial restrictions. In the face of the tremendous powers of the American capitalists and their close industrial and political union the workers of this country can win their battle only by a strong class-consciousness and closely united organizations on the economic field, a powerful and militant party on the political field and by joint attack on the common enemy.

c. That it is the duty of the Party to give moral and material support to the labor organizations in all their defensive or aggressive struggles against capitalist oppression and exploitation, for the protection and extension of the rights of the wage workers and the betterment of their material and social condition.

d. That it is the duty of the members of the Socialist Party who are eligible to membership in the unions to join and be active in their respective labor organizations.

2

Max Hayes, "Mr. Gompers' Mistake"

If the official party attitude toward existing labor unions seemed mild, the flood of writings and oratory from prominent socialists against conservative craft unionism was not. Here Max Hayes, prominent writer and labor organizer, illustrates the disdain of Samuel Gompers and his policy of collective bargaining with capitalism. From The Socialist (Perpetual) Campaign Book, 1908 (*Chicago: The Socialist Party, 1908*), *pp. 11-12.*

Capitalism controls the legislative, administrative and judicial branches of government. It dictates prices to the consumer. It defeats labor bills in congress. It legalizes the blacklist. It outlaws the boycott. It crushes strikes with injunctions, military and police. It fills trade unions with spies to destroy their effectiveness. It enforces the "open shop" and places a premium on treason to the workers. It pits female against male labor and the child against both. These indictments will not be disputed, they cannot be; they are known to every person who has eyes to see and ears to hear and brain to think.

Now what?

Political action?

Yes. It is the only means of escape left open.

But what kind of political action?

Shall it be a straight-out, manly fight through the Socialist Party, the only party that is of the workers, by the workers and for the workers, and with which the trade unionists of all other countries in the world are affiliated?

Or shall it be a guerrilla warfare of "punish our enemies and reward our friends," a plan suggested by certain national union officials without consulting the membership, an undemocratic procedure to begin with?

Or shall it continue to be the same meek, docile party slavery that is responsible for the present crisis that confronts the working people, the same child-like hope that the master class in control will throw labor a few crumbs?

This latter dog-under-the-table policy need hardly be discussed. The willing, cowardly slave never receives any consideration and probably deserves none. As a general proposition the Republican and Democratic parties have promised the workers nothing tangible to lighten the burdens piled on by capitalism and the workers usually received just what was promised, and kicks and cuffs besides.

Only a few years ago conservative folk who now urge us to "punish our enemies and reward our friends" were vociferous in claiming that the Socialists were wrong and unsound and impossible in advocating political action through a party based on working class interests, and some even declared that the unions would be able to accomplish through action on the industrial field what the Socialists aimed to do politically, viz.: gain economic emancipation for labor.

But the conservatives were wrong then and are wrong now. For years the working men have been voting for those whom they believed to be "friends," who made solemn promises before election day only to forget them the day after the polls closed. There is no assurance that that old bunco game will not be continued. At best the "friends" may be friends in one instance and enemies in the next.

It has been quite the fashion in Congress and state legislatures to pass a labor bill through one branch and pigeon-hole it in the other. The Senate passes a bill to be chloroformed in a House committee and the House railroads a bill to be killed in the Senate and then politicians in both branches go home and show that they were "friends" and voted for a labor bill or two, but the other fellows were the "enemies." Nor do the "friends" enlighten their constituents as to why they support many of the vicious corporation measures introduced.

However, more important by far than all else in this "punishing" and "rewarding" game is the danger of engendering internal controversies among the unions. Members who have been active in the Republican and Democratic parties insist that So-and-so is "our friend," others object and have their favorites, and bad feeling is aroused which proves injurious to the organization and makes foes of individual members. . . .

"Divide and conquer" has ever been the motto of the tyrant, and it can be taken for granted that the open shop fanatics will not neglect the opportunity to employ their spies in the trade unions to cause as much trouble as possible in the hair-splitting game of picking out "friends" and "enemies." . . .

The workers can never be free until they secede from the capitalist parties, stand together solidly in the Socialistic party, conquer the powers of government at the ballot box and make themselves master of the injunction bludgeon, the policeman's club and militiaman's bayonet, and enact and interpret their own laws for their own class, just as the capitalists are doing today.

The Socialist platform is plain and clear; there is no double-dealing and compromise in it. It rings true to the working class in every sentence. The Socialist party nominees require no introducton, no indorsement from labor officials.

They are labor men, union men, men who have fought the good fight with you and me, men in every sense of the word, every inch of them. . . .

3

Eugene V. Debs, "Labor in Politics"

No man attacked craft unionism more bitingly than Debs. His favorite whipping boy was Gompers, whom he never forgave for inaction during the Pullman strike, and who epitomized organized labor's cooperation with capitalism. In 1908 when Gompers broke precedent and urged A.F. of L members to support W. J. Bryan for president, and took to the stump himself to oppose both William H. Taft, the Republican nominee, and socialism, Debs issued a typical blast. From The Appeal to Reason, *January 18, 1908.*

. . . Now we have always been in favor of labor going into politics. . . . But our position differs very decidedly from that of Mr. Gompers, and since we are now approaching a national election of the greatest importance we take this occasion to address a few words to the workingmen of the United States. . . .

First, President Gompers believes that the interests of labor and capital are identical or mutual. We do not. He believes these interests can be harmonized and justice done to both. We do not. We believe labor is entitled to all it produces and that labor must organize politically as well as economically to abolish the existing order, put itself in possession of the means of production, employ itself and take to itself all it produces.

Second, Mr. Gompers does not believe in independent political action. We do. Mr. Gompers and his lieutenants have been trying for many years to procure legislation in favor of labor. They have failed miserably, utterly, and we may say, contemptibly, and they always will. . . .

Third, We are agreed with Mr. Gompers upon just one point. We do not want the unions as such to become political bodies or to be used to promote political ends. We believe in the thorough organization of the working class upon the economic field and we also believe in the thorough organization of the working class upon the political field. . . .

Fourth, . . . It is scarcely less than idiocy for labor leaders to expect these tools of capitalism [the Democratic and Republican parties] to legislate in the interests of labor. It would be as reasonable to expect a cow to bray or a mule to bark. A capitalist congress can no more change its nature than a leopard can change its spots. Mr. Gompers and his crowd use their influence to elect a capitalist congress; what right have they to object to capitalist legislation? If they want labor legislation let them turn their efforts to the election of a labor congress, as Socialists have long since done, and then they will get it and not before. . . .

We are not with Mr. Gompers in his fight on William H. Taft or any other particular capitalist politician. We are against the whole bunch, whether labelled republicans or democrats, for they stand essentially for the same system and that system is the private ownership of the means of life and the slavery of the working class. And that is precisely what President Gompers stands for and we challenge him to disprove it. . . .

Gompers has learned nothing in his twenty-five years of labor leadership. He is still hanging on to the old method of supporting good candidates before election to be kicked out by them after election and lining up his deluded followers to invite and receive the contempt of the wily politicians who have no use for working men except as they can be used to further their political ends. . . .

We appeal to the working class to quit capitalist parties of whatever name and join the Socialist Party, the only party of the working class in the United States. We appeal to every sturdy son of toil in this presidential year to cast his lot with his class and with his class strike out bravely, resolutely, unflinchingly for freedom.

4

"Gompers Replies"

Gompers had a ready answer to such socialist charges of desertion to the master class; he was building step by step for the future. Though he agreed with much of socialism, he had no use for radicalism or wild talk, which he thought retarded the whole union movement. From Proceedings Of the Twenty-Third Annual Convention of the American Federation of Labor *(Boston: A.F. of L., 1903), pp. 198-200.*

. . . Our friends, the Socialists, always when with us have an excellent conception of the trouble in our industrial life. They say, as we say, and as every intelligent man or woman says, that there are miseries which surround us. We recognize the poverty, we know the sweatshops, we can play on every string of the harp, and touch the tenderest chords of human sympathy, but while we recognize the evil and would apply the remedy, our Socialist friends would look forward to the promised land, and wait for "the sweet-by-and-by." Their statements as to economic ills are right; their conclusions and their philosophy are all askew. . . .

I want to tell you, Socialists, that I have studied your philosophy; read your works upon economics, and not the meanest of them; studied your standard works, both in English and in German—have not only read, but studied them. I have heard your orators and watched the work of your movement the world over. I have kept close watch upon your doctrines for thirty years; have been closely associated with many of you, and know what you think and what you propose. I know, too, what you have up your sleeve. And I want to say that I am entirely at variance with your philosophy. Economically, you are unsound; socially, you are wrong; industrially, you are an impossibility. . . .

5

"How Much Longer?"

But socialism's dream of a workers' party died hard, and party newspapers, writers and orators ceaselessly tried to win the labor vote. From The Chicago Daily Socialist, *February 18, 1908.*

. . . The capitalist class of America evidently propose to push their advantages to the bitter end—and it will be a BITTER END FOR THEM.

The only question is, HOW MUCH LONGER WILL THE WORKERS CONTINUE TO VOTE FOR A GOVERNMENT THAT STAMPS THEM AS OUTLAWS WHEN THEY ATTEMPT TO JOIN FOR THE DEFENSE OF THEIR INTERESTS?

How long will the trade unionists of the United States permit their masters to make the rules under which labor must fight for life with those masters?

How long before they will have the determination and energy and intelligence and courage to throw off the yoke of economic and political tyranny expressed in these decisions?

Will they wait until their officers are all in jail or are terrorized into hopelessness? Will they delay until their organizations are disrupted or emasculated?

There is something laughably tragic in the picture of the great giant Labor, with a majority of the votes in a country governed by majority rule, sitting blinking and dodging before the blows of the government he creates and supports.

How long before that giant will really wake up? He has been

turning and grumbling in his sleep, stretching his great limbs and incoherently protesting of recent months.

He is reaching out for the weapon that cannot be taken from him, and that, while he retains it, makes him omnipotent—THE BALLOT.

The workers are learning that the one place at which they can still unite in defiance of the courts to express their contempt for all the machinery of capitalism is at the BALLOT BOX. They are learning that when they are united there and cast aside all false leaders furnished by their enemies, reject all political parties owned by their masters and join hands in a political party composed of the working class, knowing no interests but that of class, and fighting unreservedly for the rulership of Labor, that there can be no such word as defeat.

Let this be the answer to the attacks that are now being made upon labor unions. Let every union hall ring with the determination to strike where no strike can be lost, to boycott where no court can interfere—to STRIKE AT THE BALLOT BOX AND DECLARE A BOYCOTT ON CAPITALISM AND ALL ITS INSTITUTIONS.

IV

Socialism and Politics

THE PAGEANTRY OF SOCIALIST POLITICS IS ENGRAVED ON THE MEMories of many Americans. Few can forget the mass meetings, the campaign trains aflame with bunting, the genial picnics with their air of devout purpose, the sense of participation while handing out leaflets or haranguing a street corner crowd. Though the socialists lacked funds for electoral crusades comparable to Democratic and Republican efforts, communal work, careful husbanding of resources, and shrewd campaigning made the party of Debs seem politically stronger than it was. Votes! was the cry, for the American loves politics. But not only votes took the socialists to the hustings. Their quadrennial presidential campaigns were educational devices to keep socialism's theory, promise, and strength alive to millions of Americans. Socialist politicking on state and local levels was an even more immediate educational device that often repaid hard work with offices and at least the appearance of some political power.

American socialism's two most famous figures, Eugene V. Debs and Norman Thomas, both ran for president. Debs stood the strain of campaigning in every election between 1900 and 1920, except for 1916 when he ran for Congress from his Indiana district. In 1920, he ran from Atlanta Federal Prison while serving a term for violating the wartime Espionage Act. Thomas ran in every presidential campaign between 1928 and 1948, and stamped his eloquence and personality on almost two generations of politically minded Americans.

It is somewhat deceptive to focus on socialism in national politics, however glamorous and colorful, for the party won electoral success at a lower level. Debs polled almost 6 per cent of the national vote in 1912, but socialist victories in city and state contests in 1910 and

45

1912 were more immediately impressive. In Milwaukee, Seattle, Butte, and other cities, the socialists were often a force in local affairs.

The pageantry and dynamism surrounding socialist presidential politics often covered strains in party unity, and Debs' greatest contribution to the movement was the unifying effect of his personality and beliefs. No socialist could argue with his human sympathy; none was unmoved by his eloquence and approach. His appearances caused hysteria among the faithful. He even partially financed his campaigns by charging admission to his meetings and speeches.

The socialists divided into roughly two groups on political philosophy. The "slowcialists," centered around Victor Berger and his successful machine in Milwaukee, wished to work methodically in politics, organizing precincts, enduring tiresome ward-heeling work. But their socialism left many dissatisfied, for it seemed no more radical than progressive Republicanism or Democracy. They argued that their goal was socialism, and the means were irrelevant. Their opponents replied that their means determined the kind of socialism they would ultimately adopt.

The radicals within the party preferred a more vital, genuinely socialistic appeal on a national as well as local level. It might be unrewarding in quick results, but in the long run it would further socialism more than bourgeois reform. Who could get excited, they said, over municipal ownership? Of what value were socialist aldermen, legislators, and mayors if they did nothing socialistic? It was dangerous to risk sliding into politics for its own sake at the expense of long term socialist goals. Where would socialist politicians lead the party if their eyes were on the next election rather than the Cooperative Commonwealth?

The party solved its problem officially by allowing each group to go its own way. The "slowcialists" won their local victories and passed reforms. The others rallied around Debs until the mid-1920's to dramatize a more radical socialism. It cost the movement much in waste motion, for the policy of compromise bred in-fighting and endless debate. Of the two views on politics, the "slowcialists" had the better practical arguments if electoral victories were important.

By adopting many tested campaign techniques, by appealing to emotion as well as reason, by trying to devise a program fitted to all classes of Americans, the socialists left a bright page in our political history. One who saw it unfold is not likely to forget it; nor is one who studies it.

1

"Immediate Demands"

The party developed and endorsed a set of immediate demands as well as long term goals, embodied in a political platform for the state and local levels. In view of the widespread acceptance of most of these ideas two generations later, the municipal program is of special interest. From The Proceedings of the National Convention of the Socialist Party, 1904 *(Chicago: The Socialist Party, 1904), pp. 318-320.*

MUNICIPAL PROGRAM

Public Education

I. Changes in Instruction

a. Sufficient kindergartens for all children of proper age.

b. Manual training (not trade schools) in all grades.

c. General introduction of idea of development and freedom in education with close connection with things, according to principles of modern pedagogy.

d. Teaching of economics and history with evolution of industry as base.

e. Establishment of vocational schools.

f. Adequate night schools for adults.

g. Instruction of children as to child labor legislation and rights of children before the law.

II. Changes Affecting Teaching Force

a. Adequate number of teachers (small classes in all schools).

b. Normal school training required as minimum qualification for teaching.

c. Right of trial for teachers before dismissal.

d. Pensions for teachers when super-annuated or disabled.

III. Care of Children

a. Uniform, free textbooks for all schools, public and private, on demand.

b. Free meals and clothing.

c. Free medical service, inspection for eyes, ears, mental faculties (for educational purposes), and for contagion.

IV. Equipment

a. Adequate buildings, numerous, not too large.

b. Ample playgrounds, with physical instructor in charge.

c. Museums, art galleries, libraries, etc., enlarged and accessible to all children through frequent visits accompanied by teachers.

d. Baths and gymnasiums in each school.

e. All school buildings open evenings, Sundays and holidays for public assemblages.

Municipal Ownership

I. Principles of Management

a. Reduction of hours and increase of wages to correspond with improvements in production.

b. No profits to be used for reduction of taxation.

c. Pension for all city employees when sick or disabled.

II. Industries Suggested for Ownership

a. All industries dependent upon franchises, such as street cars, electric and gas lighting, telephones, etc.

b. Bakeries, icehouses, coal and wood yards, department stores, slaughterhouses where they are needed.

III. Municipal Autonomy

a. Municipal autonomy for the ownership and operation of all enterprises vital to the municipality as such.

b. Issuance of bonds for this purpose up to 50 per cent of the assessed valuation.

c. Issuance of debenture bonds, secured by plants to be acquired or built.

IV. Working Class Government

a. Police not to be used in interest of employer or against strikers.

b. Free legal advice.

c. Abolition of fee system in all courts. Trial by jury without extra expense.

d. Abolition of fines as alternative to imprisonment.

e. Establishment of municipal labor bureau for investigation, inspection and report upon conditions of labor.

V. General Measures for Public Relief

a. Establishment of useful works and extension of public functions to give work to unemployed.

b. Free medical service, including free medicine.

c. Adequate hospital service with no taint of charity.

d. Homes for aged and invalid.

e. Night lodgings for men out of employment and without homes.

f. Pensions for all public employees.

g. Free public crematory.

VI. Department of Public Health

a. Inspection of food, punishment of all harmful adulteration.

b. Public disinfection after contagious diseases.

c. Publicly owned and administered baths, wash-houses, closets, laboratories, drug stores, and such other things as care of public health demands.

d. Adequate system of parks, public playgrounds, and gymnasiums.

VII. Factory Legislation

a. Special laws for protection of both women and children in both mercantile and industrial pursuits.

b. No child under 18 may be permitted to work at any gainful occupation, including selling papers, blacking shoes, etc.

VIII. Housing Question

a. Strict legislation against overcrowding, provision for light and ventilation in all rooms.

b. Building of municipal apartments to rent at cost of care of buildings and depreciation—no return for ground rent to be demanded.

c. Condemnation and destruction by the city of all tenements not conforming to proper standards of light, ventilation and overcrowding.

IX. Public Employment

a. Direct employment by the city—abolition of contract system.

b. Fixing of minimum wage not lower than standard trade union rate.

X. Taxation

a. Progressive income tax, such revenue to be used solely in the interests of the working class, and not to relieve the middle class of taxation.

b. Taxation of ground rents.

c. Exemption of household furniture and laborers' homes up to $2000.

XI. Miscellaneous

a. Erection of "Labor Temple" by municipality as headquarters, meeting place and educational center for workers of the city.

2

Victor Berger, "Socialism: The Logical Outcome of Progressivism"

This comprehensive local program was designed to provide a pattern for continued expansion and growth, solid socialist success, and assurance to all that the party was not revolutionary. Berger was the chief spokesman for this wing of the party, and looked upon such

*municipal and state programs as the only road to socialism's triumph
in America. From* American Magazine, *LXXV* (*November 1912*),
19-21.

. . . The Socialist party stands for the collective ownership of all
the social means of production and distribution in the interest of the
whole people.

Socialists say that this step is the necessary and natural outcome
of the concentration of wealth and of the development of capitalism.

Antagonists of Socialism in the past claimed that collective ownership of an industry was impossible because the personal supervision
and control of the owner was absolutely necessary to the success of
any enterprise.

To-day we see that the greatest undertakings are those in which
the stockholders and owners have nothing to do with the management of affairs and are only drawing dividends.

In all of our large industrial concerns—stock companies, railroads and trusts—business is managed and carried on by a few paid
officials. These men might just as well be paid by the state, or the
nation (as the case may be), to carry on the enterprise in the interests of the people, as paid by a few wealthy men to carry it on for
their individual profit.

Moreover, we find that whenever the nation, state or community
has undertaken to own and manage any large industry, railroad,
mine, factory, telegraph, telephone, mill, or canal, etc., this invariably redounded to the benefit of the commonwealth—the inherent
weakness of our political spoils system, notwithstanding.

This idea, carried out gradually and logically, involves a complete change of our economic and political system.

Political equality under the present system is a snare and
delusion. The wage worker who depends upon a master or upon the
master class for an opportunity to make a living is not on terms
of equality with his master.

Political liberty and economic despotism are incompatible.

The Socialist party proposes to supplement our political democracy by industrial democracy.

No one dreams of abolishing private property. On the contrary, we propose to secure private property to every citizen, to the many million men and women who under the present system have no chance of ever having any. Productive capital only is to be owned in common, by the nation, the State or the municipality as the exigencies of the case may require. Business will be carried on for use and not for profit. . . .

The Capitalist system has undoubtedly done some good in this world. The Capitalist system was useful. It has concentrated economic forces and has made possible the production of wealth on a very large scale.

The Capitalist system was a step in the evolution to freedom, but only a step. It has now outlived its usefulness. It has become oppressive to the great majority of the people. Therefore it must pass away. . . .

The Socialist party has not a majority as yet. But Socialistic ideas have permeated the great majority. The trusts and economic evolution on one hand—and the natural discontent of the people with the lowering of their standard of living on the other hand, are working for socialism.

Therefore, we laugh at the contention that the Socialist party is still comparatively small. Every great party is still comparatively small. Every great party has had a small beginning—and the Socialist party is growing exceedingly fast. . . .

To the common citizen, the working man, the underpaid clerk, the disappointed professional man,—to the disinherited of every description—we Socialists say:

Better vote for what you want, even if you do not get it, than vote for what you do not want and get it!

Why should we wait with our work until the majority of the votes is with us? The majority is always indolent and often ignorant. We cannot expect them to be anything else with their present social surroundings.

The majority have never brought about consciously and deliberately any great social change. They have always permitted an energetic minority to prepare the way. But the majority was always there when the fact itself was to be accomplished.

Therefore, our sole object in State and nation for the next few years is to elect a respectable minority of Socialists.

We want a Socialist minority respected on account of
bers,—respected because it represents the most advanced ε
and political intelligence of the day—respected because it
the most sincere representatives of the proletariat, the cl
has the most to gain and nothing to lose.

Given such a respectable minority in Congress and in the Legislature of every State of the Union within the next few years—the
future of our people, the future of this country will be safe.

3

Eugene V. Debs, "Danger Ahead"

*The left wing socialists distrusted Berger's politics, and feared that
too rapid political success tinged with reform would sweep socialism
away from its long term revolutionary goals. Their argument is well
stated here. From* The International Socialist Review, *XI (January
1911), 413-415.*

. . . The danger I see is that the Socialist party at this stage, and
under existing conditions, is apt to attract elements which it cannot
assimilate, and that it may be either weighted down, or torn asunder
with internal strife, or that it may become permeated and corrupted
with the spirit of bourgeois reform to an extent that will practically
destroy its virility and efficiency as a revolutionary organization.

To my mind the working class character and the revolutionary
integrity of the Socialist party are of first importance. All the votes
of the people would do us no good if our party ceased to be a revolutionary party, or only incidentally so, while yielding more and more
to the pressure to modify the principles and program of the party
for the sake of swelling the vote and hastening the day of its
expected triumph.

It is precisely this policy and the alluring promise it holds out to
new members with more zeal than knowledge of working class
economics that constitutes the danger we should guard against in
preparing for the next campaign. The truth is that we have not a
few members who regard vote-getting as of supreme importance, no
matter by what method the votes may be secured, and this leads

them to hold out inducements and make representations which are not at all compatible with the stern and uncompromising principles of a revolutionary party. They seek to make the socialist propaganda so attractive—eliminating whatever may give offense to bourgeoise sensibilities—that it serves as a bait for votes rather than as a means of education, and votes thus secured do not properly belong to us and do injustice to our party as well as to those who cast them.

These votes do not express socialism and in the next ensuing election are quite as apt to be turned against us, and it is better that they be not cast for the Socialist party, registering a degree of progress the party is not entitled to and indicating a political position the party in unable to sustain.

Socialism is a matter of growth, of evolution, which can be advanced by wise methods, but never by obtaining for it a fictitious vote. We should seek to register only the actual vote of socialism, no more and no less. In our propaganda we should state our principles clearly, speak the truth fearlessly, seeking neither to flatter nor to offend, but only to convince those who should be with us and win them to our cause through an intelligent understanding of its mission.

There is also a disposition on the part of some to join hands with reactionary trade unionists in local emergencies and in certain temporary situations to effect some specific purpose, which may or may not be in harmony with our revolutionary program. No possible good can come from any kind of political alliance, express or implied, with trade-unionists or the leaders of trade unions who are opposed to socialism and only turn to it for use in some extremity, the fruit of their own reactionary policy.

Of course we want the support of trade-unionists, but only of those who believe in socialism and are ready to vote and work with us for the overthrow of capitalism. . . .

Voting for socialism is not socialism any more than a menu is a meal.

Socialism must be organized, drilled, equipped and the place to begin is in the industries where the workers are employed. Their economic power has got to be developed through efficient organization, or their political power, even if it could be developed, would but react upon them, thwart their plans, blast their hopes, and all but destroy them. . . .

Now that the capitalist system is so palpably breaking down, and in consequence its political parties breaking up, the disintegrating elements with vague reform ideas and radical bourgeois tendencies will head in increasing numbers toward the Socialist party, especially since the greatly enlarged vote of this year has been announced and the party is looming up as a possible dispenser of the spoils of office. There is danger, I believe, that the party may be swamped by such an exodus and the best possible means, and in fact, the only effectual means of securing the party against such a fatality is the economic power of the industrially-organized workers.

The votes will come rapidly enough from now on without seeking them and we should make it clear that the Socialist party wants the votes only of those who want socialism, and that, above all, as a revolutionary party of the working class, it discountenances vote-seeking for the sake of votes and holds in contempt office-seeking for the sake of office. These belong entirely to capitalist parties with their bosses and their boodle and have no place in a party whose shibboleth is emancipation.

With the workers efficiently organized industrially, bound together by the common tie of their enlightened self-interest, they will just as naturally and inevitably express their economic solidarity in political terms and cast a united vote for the party of their class as the forces of nature express obedience to the laws of gravitation.

4

"Socialist Party Platform, 1912"

The party's national platforms were skillful combinations of revolutionary rhetoric and progressive reform programs, reflecting the intra-party debates between the right and left wings. The platform of 1912, when Debs received his largest vote, is typical. From Proceedings of the National Convention of the Socialist Party, 1912 (*Chicago: The Socialist Party, 1912*) , *pp. 196-198.*

. . . All political parties are the expression of economic class interests. All other parties than the Socialist party represent one or another group of the ruling capitalist class. Their political conflicts reflect merely superficial rivalries between competing capitalist groups. However they result, these conflicts have no issue of real value to the workers. Whether the Democrats or Republicans win politically, it is the capitalist class that is victorious economically.

The Socialist party is the political expression of the economic interests of the workers. Its defeats have been their defeats and its victories their victories. It is a party founded on the science and laws of social development. It proposes that, since all social necessities today are socially produced, the means of their production and distribution shall be socially owned and democratically controlled.

In the fact of the economic and political aggressions of the capitalist class the only reliance left the workers is that of their economic organization and their political power. By the intelligent and class-conscious use of these, they may resist successfully the capitalist class, break the fetters of wage-slavery, and fit themselves for the future society, which is to displace the capitalist system. The Socialist party appreciates the full significance of class organization, and urges the wage earners, the working farmers and all other useful workers everywhere to organize for economic and political action, and we pledge ourselves to support the toilers of the fields as well as those in the shops, factories and mines of the nation in their struggles for economic justice.

In the defeat or victory of the working class party in this new struggle for freedom lies the defeat or triumph of the common people of all economic groups, as well as the failure or the triumph of popular government. Thus the Socialist party is the party of the present day revolution, which marks the transition from economic individualism to socialism, from wage-slavery to free co-operation, from capitalist oligarchy to industrial democracy.

WORKING PROGRAM

As measures calculated to strengthen the working class in its fight for the realization of its ultimate aim, the co-operative commonwealth, and to increase its power of resistance to capitalist oppression, we advance and pledge ourselves and our elected officers to the following program:

Collective Ownership

a. The collective ownership and democratic management of railroads, wire and wireless telegraphs and telephones, express services, steamboat lines and all other social means of transportation and communication and of all large-scale industries.

b. The immediate acquirement by the municipalities, the states or the federal government, of all grain elevators, stockyards, storage warehouses, and other distributing agencies, in order to reduce the present extortionate cost of living.

c. The extension of the public domain to include mines, quarries, oil wells, forests, and water power.

d. The further conservation and development of natural resources for the use and benefit of all the people:

(1) By scientific forestation and timber protection.

(2) By the reclamation of arid and swamp tracts.

(3) By the storage of flood waters and the utilization of water power.

(4) By the stoppage of the present extravagant waste of the soil and of the products of mines and oil wells.

(5) By the development of highway and waterway systems.

e. The collective ownership of land wherever practicable, and in cases where such ownership is impracticable, the appropriation by taxation of the annual rental value of all land held for speculation or exploitation.

f. The collective ownership and democratic management of the banking and currency system.

Unemployment

a. The immediate government relief of the unemployed by the extension of all useful public works. All persons employed on such works to be engaged directly by the government under a workday of not more than eight hours and at not less than the prevailing union wages. The government also to establish employment bureaus; to lend money to states and municipalities without interest for the purpose of carrying on public works, and to take such other measures within its power as will lessen the widespread misery of the workers caused by the misrule of the capitalist class.

Industrial Demands

The conservation of human resources, particularly of the lives and well being of the workers and their families:

a. By shortening of the workday in keeping with the increased productiveness of machinery.

b. By securing to every worker a rest period of not less than a day and a half in each week.

c. By securing a more effective inspection of workshops, factories and mines.

d. By forbidding the employment of children under sixteen years of age.

e. By the co-operative organization of the industries in the federal penitentiaries for the benefit of the convicts and their dependents.

f. By forbidding the interstate transportation of the products of child labor, of convict labor and of all uninspected factories and mines.

g. By abolishing the profit system in government work and substituting either the direct hire of labor or the awarding of contracts to co-operative groups of workers.

h. By establishing minimum wage scales.

i. By abolishing official charity and substituting a non-contributory system of old-age pensions, a general system of insurance by the State of all its members against unemployment and invalidism and a system of compulsory insurance by employers of their workers, without cost to the latter, against industrial diseases, accidents and death.

Political Demands

a. The absolute freedom of press, speech and assembly.

b. The adoption of a graduated income tax, the increase of the rates of the present corporation tax and the extension of inheritance taxes graduated in proportion to the value of the estate and to nearness of kin—the proceeds of these taxes to be employed in the socialization of industry.

c. The abolition of the monopoly ownership of patents and the substitution of collective ownership, with direct awards to inventors by premiums or royalties.

d. Unrestricted and equal suffrage for men and women.

e. The adoption of the initiative, referendum and recall and of proportional representation, nationally as well as locally.

f. The abolition of the Senate and of the veto power of the President.

g. The election of the President and of the Vice-President by the direct vote of the people.

h. The abolition of the power usurped by the Supreme Court of the United States to pass upon the constitutionality of the legislation enacted by Congress. National laws to be repealed only by act of Congress or by a referendum vote of the whole people.

i. The abolition of the present restrictions upon the amendment of the constitution, so that instrument may be made amendable by a majority of the voters in a majority of the States.

j. The granting of the right of suffrage in the District of Columbia with representation in Congress and a democratic form of municipal government for purely local affairs.

k. The extension of democratic government to all United States territories.

l. The enactment of further measures for general education and particularly for vocational education in useful pursuits. The Bureau of Education to be made a Department.

m. The enactment of further measures for the conservation of health. The creation of an independent bureau of health, with such restrictions as will secure full liberty to all schools of practice.

n. The separation of the present Bureau of Labor from the Department of Commerce and its elevation to the rank of a department.

o. Abolition of all federal district courts and the United States circuit courts of appeals. State courts to have jurisdiction in all cases arising between citizens of the several states and foreign corporations. The election of all judges for short terms.

p. The immediate curbing of the power of the courts to issue injunctions.

q. The free administration of the law.

r. The calling of a convention for the revision of the constitution of the United States.

Such measures of relief as we may be able to force from capitalism are but a preparation of the workers to seize the whole powers of government, in order that they may thereby lay hold of the whole system of socialized industry and thus come to their rightful inheritance.

5

"The Surprising Campaign of Mr. Debs"

Debs' campaigns provoked mass hysteria among the faithful and drew national attention to socialism. In 1908 the party provided a special train, dubbed "The Red Special," in which the socialist candidate toured the country, arousing an enthusiastic following. The following report in a national non-socialist magazine gives some idea of his progress. From Current Literature, *XLV (November 1908), 481-483.*

To the country at large the one most surprising development of the campaign is the intensity of interest shown in the candidacy of Eugene V. Debs, the nominee of the Socialist party. The tremendous ovation given him in New York City last month was startling, but it was only one of similar indications seen in many parts of the country. In Boston, Faneuil Hall was packed to the doors to hear him, and three thousand persons who could not get in held an overflow meeting outdoors. A procession ten blocks long escorted him to the hall. In New Haven a similar rush for seats occurred. In New York City the demonstrations were on a scale that would have done credit to either old party in one of their greatest efforts. As Debs came into the station on his "Red Special," four thousand men and women crowded about him, "eager to touch even so much as the hem of his garment," as one of the daily papers put it. The spacious Hippodrome was packed with an audience of about 7500 persons, who had paid for admission, and who for more than three solid hours sat and waited patiently for his arrival. At the same time an overflow audience of 2500 occupied the seats of the American Theater, for which they also had paid, waiting for him there. After his speech at the Hippodrome, as he started to go to his hotel, so runs the account, "wildly enthusiastic Socialists tried to pick up the automobile in which he was riding, and to carry or drag it—no one could tell which—through the streets." At the dinner in his honor in the evening, women took off their jewels and contributed them to the campaign funds, this, too, after a collection of $600 had been taken up in the afternoon. Two hundred thousand persons, it is said, have contributed to the fund called for by Debs to keep his special train going to the end of the campaign.

"Comrades," began Debs, "this is our year. This year will be historic. It will mark the entrance of Socialism into the arena of national politics. Only a few years ago the smallest hall was too large for a Socialist meeting; now the largest hall is too small. It is the same everywhere. Two weeks ago we were on the Pacific coast. The audiences there were so vast that the largest auditorium had not half enough capacity to hold them." There is nothing in Debs or his oratory that will account for this enthusiasm that he arouses, tho [sic] he is by all accounts an interesting and lovable man. Lincoln Steffens describes him as "the kindest, foolishest, most courageous lover of man in the world." He is looked upon by the Socialists themselves as a sort of Don Quixote of the cause. "When Debs speaks a harsh word," says Horace Traubel, one of his admirers, "it is wet with tears." Nor is he a novelty, for he has been a presidential candidate as many times as Mr. Bryan. It is not Debs the orator, but Debs the apostle that receives these ovations that have startled the metropolitan press. Debs is clearly conscious of that fact. He admits that he is not fitted, either by temperament or by taste, for the office of President. "If there were any chance of my election," he told Steffens, "I wouldn't run. The Party wouldn't let me." The enthusiasm of this great Socialist meeting, remarked the New York *World,* referring to the Hippodrome gathering, "was not for its candidate but for its cause." . . .

6

"Uncanny, the Debs Effect"

*The Los Angeles Times, September 11, 1908, gives a vivid account
of the qualities that made Debs a successful campaigner, and of the
excitement that surrounded his meetings, even though the reporter
did not like Debs or his cause.*

Debs, the candidate of the "Reds" for President of the United
States, talked last night to a large audience of his people at the
Shrine Auditorium.

It was almost uncanny. There was something strange and un-
wholesome about his hoarse cries against Fate—it amounted to that.

Debs has a face that looks like a death's-head—great peering
eyes that stare roundly from caves under brows that twitch and flex
under queer snaky movements as he talks. A low shabby collar was
twisted tightly about his stringy neck and seemed to accentuate the
tense deep lines of his face. His head is peeled of hair on the top
and seemed, with its thin fringe at the sides, like a shining naked
skull topping the cadaverous face.

As the arch "Red" talked, he was bent at the hips like an old, old
man, his eerie face peering up and out at the audience like some
old necromancer reading a charm.

It was a hot night. Perspiration stood out on his white set face; it
rolled down until a glistening drop hung depended from his nose.
He shook it off as a horse shakes off an obstinate fly. It grew
warmer. Beads of perspiration stood out all over his face. As his
body shook with the passion of his class hatred, these drops of sweat
sometimes flew off in tiny showers.

Sometimes he seemed like a man in the shadow of death. You
could hear his breath drawn in great gasps; his [words] were
forced out past his deformed, ill-shapened teeth, in labored gusts.

Debs talks in epigrams. It is as though he were gathering himself
each time to hurl a brick.

They were mostly hurled at the political parties; the Democrats
got the worst abuse.

There were other speeches; they were ridiculous.

All the reds were trying to be as bad as they possibly could. They had an old red flag fastened onto a picture of Carl [sic] Marx. They sang "the Marseillaise" out of tune and sat with an air of firm determination as though to say, "There: maybe we're not regular devils, huh?" But they were only very tame, after all.

The only real ferocity was shown by a German singing society, which did terrible execution. They caused one to dread with renewed terror the dangers of revolution. . . .

A gentleman with a loud yawp introduced Debs. He took so long about it that the audience finally had to howl him down. While he spouted his brother socialists kept rushing out on the platform, and begging him to sit down, but he shook them off and spieled on, simply drunk with delight at the sound of his own voice.

Debs finally got the floor. He stepped to the front and looked out over the audience with a ghastly, mirthless smile. "A tribute," he said sardonically, "to an undesirable citizen."

He suddenly lashed into the Republican party, accusing it of responsibility for the panic of last October.

"Eight years ago," he said, "their party slogan was, 'Let well enough alone.' Four years ago their slogan was 'Stand Pat.' This year their slogan is 'God knows.' "

He turned onto Taft.

"When you find yourselves out of employment," he cried passionately, "when you find yourselves on the verge of starvation, you ask your Republican candidate for President what you are to do, [and] he refers you to the Almighty. But he takes your votes himself."

After a lot of the usual socialistic talk about "wage-slaves," he said: "This year will be historic. The workers are awakening. They are beginning to understand that their interests are identical. They are beginning to understand that, when united, no power on earth can stop them; when separated, they are powerless.

"About this time, every four years," he continued sarcastically, "the capitalist politicians begin to be happy to be in your presence. They begin to be impressed with your intelligence. They notice that beads of sweat upon your brows are more priceless than the jewels of a queen's coronet; but we notice that they don't wear any of that sort of jewelry themselves.

"They speak to you as the horny hands of labor. They congratulate you on your deformed hands. They congratulate you, but they know those hands are an impeachment on your intelligence."

He got off some epigrammatic comparisons of the two old-line parties.

"The Republicans believe in preserving the system as it is; the Democrats want to have it as it was."

"The Republicans suspend the laws of evolution; the Democrats reverse them."

"You are a Republican because your father was. Your father had some excuse; you have none. He joined when it was a great party, swept into power by a great issue."

"You are a Democrat because your grandfather was one. Well, everything has been changed except the grandson."

"The Democrats propose to you to guarantee your bank deposits. How many of you are worrying about your bank deposits? What you are looking for is the guarantee of a job."

"The Republican convention at Chicago was composed of plutocrats, politicians and parasites."

Voice from the audience: "And Gompers."

Debs said the Democratic convention didn't suit him any better. He made a passionate and tremendous onslaught against the Democrats, making a parade of alleged friendship for the working people and then permitting the hideous child labor of the southern factories.

He then turned onto the inevitable "wrongs of the working class," which he treated without particular bitterness.

"For countless centuries," he said, "you have been the lower class. You have built palaces and lived in cottages; you have built automobiles and walked. You have manufactured guns and have always been on the wrong end of them. You are the sovereign citizens; but think of sovereigns looking for jobs."

He turned contemptuously onto capital. "We don't want your paltry capital," he cried. "We want the earth. You need not worry about us. We won't hurt you. Your capitalistic competitors will attend to you. Then you will be ready to join us and help us dispossess the dispossessors.

"Capital," he said, "has served its mission. Capitalism has solved the problem of developing wealth. Socialism will solve the problem of distributing it."

7

"The Socialist Vote in 1912"

The party polled its largest percentage of national votes in 1912. They are arranged below by state, both in number and percentage of the total state vote. From The Socialist Congressional Campaign Book, 1914 (*Chicago: Socialist Party, 1914*), *pp. 19-20.*

State	Vote	Percentage
Alabama	3,029	2.57
Arizona	3,163	13.33
Arkansas	8,153	6.57
California	79,201	11.76
Colorado	16,418	6.16
Connecticut	10,056	5.28
Delaware	556	1.14
Florida	4,806	9.26
Georgia	1,028	.85
Idaho	11,960	11.31
Illinois	81,249	7.09
Indiana	36,931	5.64
Iowa	16,967	3.45
Kansas	26,779	7.33
Kentucky	11,647	2.35
Louisiana	5,249	6.61
Maine	2,541	1.96
Maryland	3,996	1.72
Massachusetts	12,662	2.59
Michigan	23,211	4.23
Minnesota	27,505	8.33
Mississippi	2,061	3.19
Missouri	28,466	4.04
Montana	10,885	13.66
Nebraska	10,185	4.09
Nevada	3,313	16.61
New Hampshire	1,980	2.25
New Jersey	15,928	3.68

New Mexico	2,859	5.79
New York	63,381	3.99
North Carolina	1,025	.42
North Dakota	6,966	8.04
Ohio	89,930	8.70
Oklahoma	42,262	16.61
Oregon	13,343	9.74
Pennsylvania	83,614	6.65
Rhode Island	2,049	2.63
South Carolina	164	.33
South Dakota	4,662	4.01
Tennessee	3,504	1.41
Texas	24,896	8.25
Utah	9,023	8.03
Vermont	928	1.48
Virginia	820	.60
Washington	40,134	12.43
West Virginia	15,336	5.71
Wisconsin	33,481	8.37
Wyoming	2,760	6.52

8

Morris Hillquit, "Problems and Prospects of American Socialism"

As usual, Hillquit analyzed socialism's political position in America with considerable shrewdness and objectivity. From History of Socialism in the United States, *5th ed. (New York: Funk & Wagnalls Co., 1910), pp. 358-365. By permission of Mrs. Sylvia Angrist.*

. . . The Socialist movement in this country has thus made substantial gains within the last decade. It has begun to penetrate the broad masses of American workingmen, has enlisted the support of many persons in other classes, and has spread to all parts of the country. But with all that the progress of socialism in the United States has even within that period, been slower than in almost any other civilized country. The difficulties which beset the path of the American socialists are varied and many. . . .

Although the modern or "capitalist" system of production is at present probably more highly developed in the United States than in any other country, the development is of comparatively recent

date. Only one generation ago agriculture was the main industry of
the country while manufacture was conducted on a comparatively
small scale. This condition, together with the relative prosperity of
the country generally, operated to retard the formation of a permanent wage-working class, the existence of which is essential to
the growth of the modern socialist movement. . . .

Another obstacle has been the political system of the country.
Paradoxical as it may seem, our very democracy has militated against
the immediate success of socialism. The tremendous number of our
elective offices, with their great powers and patronage, have made
the politics of our country a matter of extraordinary importance.
The political campaigns of the United States exceed those of all
other countries in intensity and dimensions. Politics has become as
much an industry with us as railroading or manufacturing. It is
conducted by professionals for their private gain, on a large scale
and with a lavish outlay of capital. Our political campaigns are
more often struggles of individuals for office than contests of masses
over principles. Perhaps nowhere in the world is there less political
idealism and more political corruption. . . .

The difficulties of all . . . reform movements are still more ag-
gravated by the so-called "two-party" system in American politics.
Ever since the creation of the republic the contest for political
power has been waged between two, and only two, dominant parties.
New political parties, so-called "third parties," have appeared in the
arena from time to time, but not one of them has developed any
appreciable strength and stability. As a rule they have, after a more
or less tempestuous career, been absorbed by one of the old
parties. . . .

But what makes it [American politics] still more difficult is the
system of "party tickets" in elections. . . . Local, state and national
elections are most frequently held together, and the ticket handed
to the voter sometimes contains the names not only of candidates
for the state legislature or congress, but also for all local and state
officers and even for President of the United States. And since a new
party rarely seems to have the chance or prospect of electing its candidate for governor or president of the country, the voter is inclined
in advance to consider its entire ticket as hopeless. The fear
of "throwing away" the vote is thus a peculiar product of American

politics, and it requires a voter of exceptional strength of conviction to overcome it.

Another and perhaps not less serious obstacle to the growth of political socialism in the United States is our system of state autonomy. The main socialist program, as well as the most important immediate reforms advocated by the socialists, can be realized only on a national scale. In every country it is always some concrete demand addressed to the national legislature, the parliament, which unites the masses of the population into one solid reform or revolutionary movement. In the United States where the powers and scope of the national government are exceedingly limited, and the most vital industrial and social problems of the country are left to be dealt with by the 46 different and independent legislatures of our States, general social reform movements have to traverse a much more difficult road.

Nor are the ethnic conditions of the country very favorable to the growth of socialism. . . . By far the greater part of [the immigrants] are workers, and they are, of necessity, a factor of greater importance for the socialist movement than they would be for a reform movement of the middle classes. The Socialist Party in the United States is compelled to address the workers of the country in more than twenty different languages and to adjust its organization and methods of propaganda to the conditions and habits of more than twenty different races. The presence of about nine million negroes, mostly workers, with special racial and social conditions, raises another very serious problem for the socialist movement in this country. All these factors indicate but do not exhaust the peculiar difficulties of American socialism. Will these difficulties prove insurmountable?

The entire history of socialism militates against such a conclusion. . . . Its progress has been rapid or slow, even or irregular, according to the special conditions of each country, but progress there has been in all countries, and very decided progress in the long run. For socialism is primarily and mainly a product of modern industrial conditions. It appeared with the appearance of these conditions and it is growing with their growth. The present or "capitalist" mode of production makes necessary the rise of a permanent, large and growing wage-working class, engaged in an ever fiercer struggle for existence and consciously or instinctively forced into organized resistance against the employing classes. This resistance uniformly assumes the form of an economic and political struggle of the working class, for paltry benefits at first, for more radical reforms subsequently, and ultimately for the complete abolition of the oppressive industrial system. This is the logic of war and the history of all struggles of the masses. . . .

A tactful policy and energetic work on the part of the organized socialists, in the direction indicated, may largely accelerate the progress of the movement; unwise methods or lack of action may retard it somewhat. American socialism has not as yet evolved definite and settled policies and methods. The movement is largely in the making, but the more recent phases of its development tend to indicate that it is beginning to solve its problems and overcome its obstacles. Slow as has been the progress of political socialism in this country, it has made larger gains within the last ten years than within all the thirty or forty years preceding that period. The vote and the enrolled membership of the Socialist Party have grown almost five-fold, and the socialists have gained an important political standing in some sections of the country. Furthermore, there is every reason to believe that the latent political strength of socialism is much larger than the socialist vote would indicate. . . .

Nor are the political achievements of socialism the sole, or even the most important, test of the growth of the movement. In its present phase, socialism in this country is primarily an educational movement, and as such it has made its greatest gains within recent years. It has succeeded in dispelling many of the grosser popular prejudices against the movement, and has created a more enlightened, tolerant, and sympathetic attitude toward its general aims and methods. Many of the measures of industrial, social, and political reform, originally advocated exclusively by the socialists, are gradually being forced into the platform of other parties and organizations. The socialist program has become one of the favorite topics of discussion in books, in the periodical press, and on our public platforms. Socialism is at last beginning to get a hearing before the people, and the people of the United States move fast when once they are set in motion.

V

Socialism and Special Interest Groups

THE SOCIALISTS KNEW THAT TO SUCCEED EITHER POLITICALLY OR ECO-
nomically they must make their movement a coalition of sometimes
conflicting interest groups. It was easy to appeal to labor, for the
worker's future gains under socialism could be made as enticing as
his present discomfort was real. But it was another matter to make
socialism appealing to American farmers, always rugged individualists; to American intellectuals, often suspicious of radicalism; to the
youthful middle class, which though possessing a social conscience
still wished to partake of America's material rewards. And how
could the socialists reach the inarticulate submerged masses who
might often as not be dead weight to the movement? Could they
welcome the Negroes, the immigrants, the downtrodden without
sacrificing further their precarious party unity? Every special group
added meant another voice in the movement's councils.

It was a difficult task which has confounded many movements in
American history, but the socialists accomplished much in their
building before World War I. They based their appeal on the
general assumption that all groups were interdependent; cooperation not competition was the keynote of both individual and collective success. Without offering special favors on any significant
scale, they managed to blend their humanitarian appeal with the
realities of economics and politics to win support from some special
groups.

SOCIALISM AND THE NEGRO

The colored man was a logical candidate for admission into the
socialist utopia. He was oppressed in every sphere of life—segre-

gated socially, discriminated against economically, politically mute. His situation outraged socialist humanitarian feelings. Yet it is difficult to define the party's "attitude" toward the problem because the socialists did not devise a special program for the persecuted Negro. That would have violated the belief that capitalism persecuted all men; the Negro's lot was harder merely because the capitalist system had singled him out for obvious historical and social reasons.

Not all socialists agreed on the Negro's status or importance to the movement. Some men like Julius Wayland, publisher of the influential newspaper *The Appeal to Reason,* frankly believed in segregation. Even Victor Berger, staunch social democrat, thought the Negro racially inferior. These men were not racists or bigots; the problem was simply unreal to them. The Negro received few benefits from the whole progressive movement, and it is not surprising that he stood outside the pale in some socialists' thinking.

But other socialist leaders urged a militant appeal to the Negro, not merely for humanitarian reasons, but to end his economic exploitation that hurt the whole labor movement. Debs bitterly denounced white treatment of the Negro, and William English Walling, prominent socialist writer and lecturer, helped found the NAACP.

Though the socialists produced no special program for the Negro, they did him the justice of seeing his plight in human terms. He was part of the larger human dilemma of his time. If his status seemed to them merely a heightened form of capitalism's "wage-slavery," they did not deny him final admission to their utopia. Judged in proper perspective, the socialists did their best to invite the Negro to partake of the goodness and to bear the badness of mankind's struggle toward a better world.

1

Eugene V. Debs, "The Negro in the Class Struggle"

The following article breathes Debs' sense of outrage over the color question and expresses the attitude of the left wing socialists.

From The International Socialist Review, *IV* (*November 1903*), 257-260.

. . . At Yoakum, Texas, a few days ago, leaving the depot with two grips in my hands, I passed four or five bearers of the white man's burden perched on a railing and decorating their environment with tobacco juice. One of them, addressing me, said: "There's a nigger that'll carry your grips." A second one added: "That's what he's here for," and a third chimed in with "That's right, by God." Here was a savory bouquet of white superiority. One glance was sufficient to satisfy me that they represented all there is of justification of the implacable hatred of the Negro race. They were ignorant, lazy, unclean, totally devoid of ambition, themselves the foul product of the capitalist system and held in lowest contempt by the master class, yet esteeming themselves immeasureably above the cleanest, most intelligent and self-respecting Negro, having by reflex absorbed the "nigger" hatred of their masters. . . .

The whole world is under obligation to the Negro, and that the white heel is still upon the black neck is simply proof that the world is not yet civilized.

The history of the Negro in the United States is a history of crime without parallel.

Why should the white man hate him? Because he stole him from his native land and for two centuries and a half robbed him of the fruit of his labor, kept him in beastly ignorance, and subjected him to the brutal domination of the lash? Because he tore the black child from the breast of its mother and ravished the black man's daughter before her father's eyes? . . .

But of all the senseless agitation in capitalist society, that in respect to "social equality" takes the palm. . . .

Social equality forsooth! Is the black man pressing his claims for social recognition upon his white burden bearer? Is there any reason why he should? Is the white man's social recognition of his own white brother such as to excite the Negro's ambition to covet the noble prize? Has the Negro any greater desire, or is there any reason why he should have, for social intercourse with the white man than the white man has for social relations with the Negro? This phase of the Negro question is pure fraud and serves to mask the real issue, which is not *social equality,* BUT ECONOMIC FREEDOM.

There never was any social inferiority that was not the shrivelled fruit of economic inequality.

The Negro, given economic freedom, will not ask the white man any social favor; and the burning question of "social equality" will disappear like mist before the sunrise.

I have said and say again that, properly speaking, there is no Negro question outside of the labor question—the working class struggle. Our position as socialists and as a party is perfectly plain. We have simply to say: "The class struggle is colorless." The capitalists, white, black, and other shades, are on one side and the workers, white, black, and all other colors, on the other side. . . .

Socialists should with pride proclaim their sympathy with and fealty to the black race, and if there be any who hesitate to avow themselves in the face of ignorant and unreasoning prejudice, they lack the true spirit of the slave-destroying revolutionary movement.

The voice of socialism must be as inspiring music to the ears of those in bondage, especially the weak black brethren, doubly enslaved, who are bowed to earth and groan in despair beneath the burdens of centuries.

For myself, my heart goes to the Negro and I make no apology to any white man for it. In fact, when I see the poor, brutalized, outraged black victim, I feel a burning sense of guilt for his intellectual poverty and moral debasement that makes me blush for the unspeakable crimes committed by my own race. . . .

2

Clarence Meily, "Socialism and the Negro Problem"

The following article represents best the general attitude of most socialists toward the Negro issue. From The International Socialist Review, *IV (November 1903), 265-267.*

Again and again it seems necessary to reiterate that socialism is merely an economic reform, and affects only indirectly and incidentally questions of a political, social, and ethical character. For the problem of race prejudice, as for that of intemperance and the "social evil," depending largely on individual culture for solution, socialism is no specific. By furnishing an improved environment, it may facilitate individual culture and so become an important factor in the working out of the answers which the future holds concealed, but were socialism realized tomorrow these questions, sinister and ominous as ever, would still confront the American people.

The prejudice against the colored man in America has two causes; the first sectional and no longer operative, though its effects persist; the second universal, active, and of economic origin. The first of these is the quondam status of the Negro as a slave, and of his white associate as master. . . . Here time, bringing with it the culture of the individual, alone can aid. And the culture needed is not merely that of the colored man, but of the white man also. The white man must learn that, real as his feelings of repulsion for his black brother may be, it is a base and ignoble thing, an occasion not of pride but of shame, a blemish in his character not to be fostered but to be eradicated. . . .

Obviously with all this socialism has nothing whatever to do. It cannot compel one man to admit another to his house, seat him at his table, or marry him to his daughter. Nor can it on the other hand curb that pragmatic spirit which leads one man, afflicted with a race prejudice, to impose it by law or social convention on his fellows. Matters of this sort are ethical, and may become political, but they are certainly not economic.

The second occasion of prejudice against the Negro operates in the breast of the white wage-earner, and arises from the presence of the colored man as a competitor in the field of labor. A glance at the conduct of mobs, North and South, when bent on Negro punishment, will serve to differentiate this from the cause first mentioned. In the South the mob, composite in character, captures and murders a single victim and disperses peaceably, the Negro community, if non-resistant, suffering comparatively slight perturbation. In the North the mob, made up almost invariably from the proletariat, using the punishment of some particular criminal as an excuse, hastens on to a general persecution and race war. . . . Under capitalism, with the surfeit of labor which it engenders, each ad-

ditional competitor in the labor market, constrained by necessity
to offer his labor power for the bare price of sustenance . . . becomes an embarrassment and menace to every other laborer. This
is particularly true in the case of the Negro, whose scale of living is
generally lower than that of the white. As he can, and will, work for
less wages, so proportionately is the animosity of his white fellow-
worker kindled against him; and it is more unfortunate than strange
if, schooled in a system which has as its keynote fratricidal strife,
the white laborer resorts to violence to rid himself of a competition
threatening his own livelihood. Here the ameliorating effect of
socialism is immediately apparent. When cooperation among laborers is substituted for competition, and the consequence of added
numbers is merely to shorten the hours of toil for all, without
any decrease of compensation to any, the colored laborer will be
welcomed as a brother, not reviled as a "scab"; will be hailed as a
fortunate accession to the armies of industry, not dreaded as a club
ready to the hand of the employer to coerce refractory employees. . . .

Lastly, what should be the attitude of the socialist to the Negro
problem? And here there must be no doubt, or cavil, or temporiz-
ing, or subterfuge, or uncertainty. For very shame, the ethics of
socialism dare not be inferior to those of the bourgeoisie which socialism supplants; and the bourgeoisie in its victory over the
noblesse having overthrown all distinctions of birth, socialism dare
not revive it. Absolute economic equality for white and black, cov-
ering perfect uniformity not only in opportunities for labor, but
also in all those public services, such as education, transportation
(including, let it be added, hotel accommodations), entertainment,
etc., which may be collectively rendered, together with complete
recognition of political rights, must be insisted on more strenu-
ously by the socialist than ever they could have been by any aboli-
tionist agitator. No "segregation of races," or other claptrap "solution," can be entertained for a moment. The drawing of invidious
caste distinctions must be left to the private individual alone in
his private affairs. . . . If now, socialism, which is the economic
victory of the working class, countenances and preserves a distinction of race, that is, a caste distinction, so far from accomplishing a
final triumph and perfecting human solidarity, it will be but a par-

tial success, nursing further injustice and further revolt. And how can socialism, the champion of the proletariat, which by classic inclusion embraces not merely the workers, but the criminals, and all the despised and rejected of the earth, recognize any distincton of race, or color, or birth, or faith amongst its children? To ask the question should be to answer it.

SOCIALISM AND THE IMMIGRANT

Like the Negro, the immigrant was an ideal candidate for socialist indoctrination. His great numbers were enticing, as was his supposed recollection of socialist strength in his mother country. Many American socialists were first or second generation immigrants. Capitalism exploited the immigrant when he sought a job. He felt the social injustice of life in ghettos. What attachment did he have to a corrupt political system that often merely used his vote against him? Many radical socialists argued that it would be a delicious irony to defeat capitalism by using its submerged masses, the system causing its own downfall.

Hard facts and theories combined to make immigration a heated issue. Conservative socialists feared immigrant radicalism; true, they argued, the immigrant had little attachment to America as yet, but what attachment could he have to socialism? He was too often ignorant, unskilled, and docile. Other socialists opposed any special treatment of immigrants within the party.

Victor Berger, himself an immigrant, and other conservatives noted the bitter fact that the immigrant was a strike breaker. His lack of skills and large numbers often depressed the labor movement. It was foolish to argue that immigrants or their children were automatically ripe for socialism. Though Berger hotly opposed restrictions on immigration, except from the Orient, he counselled patient education among immigrant groups to attain the party's ends.

The socialists faced the issue in a famous fight at the First National Congress in 1910. Berger's group favored exclusion of Orientals and contract labor. A minority report opposed contract labor but ignored the question of Orientals, since they were negligible in number, and it did not wish to offend any minority group. A compromise report, written by Hillquit, passed, favoring unrestricted immigration except where it helped capitalism.

As usual, there was more behind the intra-party quarrel than surface facts. The conservatives did not wish large numbers of immigrants to add to the party's foreign taint; this might drive off "sound" support from other groups. Who knew how radical the immigrant might be? The left wing socialists favored full immigration and a large party program to develop this fund of radicalism.

The National Congress of 1910 permitted the establishment of special foreign language federations within the party. In 1917 when the country went to war, over a third of the party's membership came from these federations. Many of them were fairly wealthy, owning real estate, newspapers, and collecting substantial dues from members. The World War divided them, and when the smoke cleared they were gone.

The socialists misjudged the importance of the immigrant. He counted heavily in small pockets like Milwaukee. On the whole, he had little affinity for socialism. Like all newcomers, he wished chiefly to conform to his changed status. The socialist dream of acquiring the immigrant failed. In the end, he preferred to join another Americanism.

1

"A Letter from Debs on Immigration"

Debs' viewpoint expresses the radical stand on immigration, couched in his usual fiery words and bitter phrases. From The International Socialist Review, *XI (July 1910), 16-17.*

[I] have just read the majority report of the Committee on Immigration. It is utterly unsocialistic, reactionary, and in truth outrageous, and I hope you will oppose it with all your power. The plea that certain races are to be excluded because of tactical expediency would be entirely consistent in a bourgeois convention of self-seekers, but should have no place in a proletariat gathering under the auspices of an international movement that is calling on the oppressed and exploited workers of all the world to unite for their emancipation. . . .

Away with the "tactics" which require the exclusion of the oppressed and suffering slaves who seek these shores with the hope of bettering their wretched condition and are driven back under the cruel lash of expediency by those who call themselves Socialists in the name of a movement whose proud boast it is that it stands uncompromisingly for the oppressed and downtrodden of all the earth. These poor slaves have just as good a right to enter here as even the authors of this report who now seek to exclude them. The only difference is that the latter had the advantage of a little education and had not been so cruelly ground and oppressed, but in point of principle there is no difference, the motive of all being precisely the same, and if the convention which meets in the name of Socialism should discriminate at all it should be in favor of the miserable races who have borne the heaviest burdens and are most nearly crushed to the earth.

Upon this vital proposition I would take my stand against the world and no specious argument of subtle and specious defenders or sophistical defenders of the civic federation unionism, who do not hesitate to sacrifice principles for numbers and jeopardize ultimate success for immediate gain, could move me to turn my back upon the oppressed, brutalized, and despairing victims of the old world, who are lured to these shores by some faint glimmer of hope that here their crushing burdens may be lightened, and some star of promise rise in their darkened skies.

The alleged advantages that would come to the Socialist movement because of such heartless exclusion would all be swept away a thousand times by the sacrifice of a cardinal principle of the international Socialist movement, for well might the good faith of such a movement be questioned by the intelligent workers if it placed itself upon record as barring its doors against the very races most in need of relief, and extinguishing their hope, and leaving them in dark despair at the very time their ears were first attuned to the international call and their hearts were beginning to throb responsive to the solidarity of the oppressed of all lands and all climes beneath the skies.

In this attitude there is nothing of maudlin sentimentality, but simply a rigid adherence to the fundamental principles of the international proletarian movement. If Socialism, international, revolutionary Socialism, does not stand staunchly, unflinchingly, and uncompromisingly for the working class and for the exploited and oppressed masses of all lands, then it stands for none and its claim is a false pretense and its profession a delusion and a snare.

Let those desert us who will because we refuse to shut the international door in the faces of their own brethren; we will be none the weaker but all the stronger for their going, for they evidently have no clear conception of the international solidarity, are wholly lacking in the revolutionary spirit, and have no proper place in the Socialist movement while they entertain such aristocratic notions of their own superiority.

Let us stand squarely on our revolutionary, working class principles and make our fight openly and uncompromisingly against all our enemies, adopting no cowardly tactics and holding out no false hopes, and our movement will then inspire the faith, arouse the spirit, and develop the fiber that will prevail against the world.

2

Morris Hillquit, "Immigration in the United States"

With a heavier pen but greater logic and less emotion than Debs, Hillquit explained the socialist stand on immigration. From The International Socialist Review, *VIII (August 1907), 65-75.*

. . . As a rule the socialists of the United States do not share the narrower views of pure and simple trade unionism on the question of immigration. . . . The immigrant workingman certainly swells the supply of labor power but to some extent he also helps to increase the demand for it. He is not only a producer, he is also a consumer, and while under the present system he is bound to consume less than he produces, it is still a gross error to overlook his stimulating effect on the industrial growth of the country. The immigrant's low standard of living is also often a temporary rather than a permanent condition. . . .

And to the extent to which immigration actually is an evil to the working class of the receiving country, it is an evil inseparable from the existing economic system, as inseparable from it as the evils of child labor or woman labor, or the existence of the standing "natural" army of unemployed workingmen in every country with a capitalist development.

The migration of workingmen is caused and regulated largely by economic conditions, it is just as much a part of our industrial order as the movement of the masses from the village to the city and from city to city within every country. . . . The efforts of organized labor should, therefore, be directed toward the organization and elevation of their immigrated brethren rather than towards their exclusion.

But if the socialists are thus unable to share all the current views of organized labor on immigration, they can just as little afford to ignore all their views. . . . Immigration artificially stimulated for the benefit of steamship companies, land agents and similar commercial concerns, is just as pernicious to the workingmen of the country of emigration as to those of the receiving country, and should be discouraged with all means at the command of the socialists and workingmen of all countries. The international importation of workingmen from foreign countries for the purpose of breaking strikes or weakening or destroying labor organizations, is just as obnoxious to socialists as it is to the trade unions, and all measures to check these capitalist practices have the full support of the socialists. And finally the majority of the American socialists side with the trade unions in their demand for the exclusion of workingmen of such races and nations as have as yet not been drawn into the sphere of modern production, and who are incapable of assimilation with the workingmen of the country of their adoption, and of joining the organizations and struggles of their class. This demand is a direct expression of the natural instinct of self-preservation. . . .

3

"The Socialist Party on Immigration"

The majority report adopted in 1910 was a beautiful example of the art of eating cake and having it too. Each paragraph mollified a major party group. From Proceedings of the First National Party Congress . . . 1910 *(Chicago: Socialist Party, 1910), see pp. 75-80, 98, 168.*

The Socialist Party favors all legislative measures tending to prevent the immigration of strike breakers and contract laborers, and the mass importation of workers from foreign countries, brought about by the employing classes for the purpose of weakening the organization of American labor, and of lowering the standards of life of American workers.

The party is opposed to the exclusion of any immigrants on account of their race or nationality, and demands that the United States be at all times maintained as a free asylum for all men and women persecuted by the governments of their countries on account of their politics, religion, or race.

SOCIALISM AND THE FARMER

It seemed at first glance that socialism offered the farmer little. The party's message could be made real to the worker and city dweller, but what would make it appealing to the rural dweller? What did socialism owe the farmer, who was traditionally (except in the South) a Republican and an upholder of capitalism in his rugged individualism?

Curiously, socialism made headway in many farm states. Oklahoma was usually near the top of the party's electoral column. California, then heavily agricultural, was receptive to socialist agitation. The Midwest, where worker and farmer might make common cause, was always restless. Party conventions drew both city and country delegates. The bowler hat and the snapping gallus both symbolized socialism's appeal. The socialists foresaw the farmers' modern dilemma of overproduction long before the farmers did.

The socialist farm program, to which the party clung tenaciously during the long slump of the 1920's and 1930's, grew with the years into a rational ideal. But the farmer found it hard to forget the party's basic orientation toward labor and the city. With the exception of various pockets of support, the socialists never claimed a widespread following among the farm population.

1

"What Socialism Will Do For The Farmer"

The following excerpt from the party's campaign book of 1912 outlines the socialist stand on the issue. From Socialist Campaign Book, 1912 *(Chicago: Socialist Party, 1912), p. 43.*

. . . The Socialist Party proposes to do all in its power to alleviate the condition of the farmer who now works with his own hands on his little bit of land; but it is not blind to the fact that all the Socialists or anyone else could do would not protect him in that ownership against the powerful forces that are taking his farm from him. So the party comes forward with the proposal that the producers of wealth on the farm shall join with those of the factory to obtain the ownership of the things necessary to their lives.

Just as the Socialist Party proposes to restore the ownership of the factory and mill, the mines and the railroads to those who work in them and who create wealth through their use, so it proposes to restore the lands and the machinery to the men who produce the crops of this country. But this cannot be individual ownership in either case; so the Socialist Party believes the time has now come for the beginning of socially-operated farms; these farms would be sufficiently large to use the most improved machinery; they would be officered and directed by the socially-trained graduates of our agricultural educational institutions and their wealth would all go to those who produced it and worked upon the farm.

Pending the time when such farms can be established, the following program adopted at our National Convention pledges the party to the enactment of a series of measures especially designed to afford relief to the great class of workers on the farm:

a. The Socialist Party demands that the means of transportation and storage and the plants used in the manufacture of farm products and farm machinery shall be socially owned and democratically managed.

b. To prevent the holding of land out of use and to eliminate tenantry, we demand that all farm land not cultivated by owners shall be taxed at its full rental value, and that actual use and occupancy shall be the only title to land.

c. We demand the retention by the national, state or local governing bodies of all land owned by them, and the continuous acquirement of other land by reclamation, purchase, condemnation, taxation or otherwise; such land to be organized as rapidly as possible into socially operated farms for the conduct of collective agricultural enterprises.

d. Such farms should constitute educational and experimental centers for crop culture, the use of fertilizers and farm machinery, and distributing points for improved seeds and better breeds of animals.

e. The formation of cooperative associations for agricultural purposes should be encouraged.

f. Insurance against diseases of animals and plants, insect pests and natural calamities should be provided by national state or local governments.

g. We call attention to the fact that the elimination of farm tenantry and the development of socially owned and operated agriculture will open new opportunities to the agricultural wage-worker and free him from the tyranny of the private employer.

2

Oscar Ameringer, "Saving the World"

Ameringer was the party's best and most imaginative evangelist among the Oklahoma farmers. His campaign techniques mixed the quilting bee with the Cooperative Commonwealth. From If You

Don't Weaken (*New York: Holt, Rinehart & Winston, Inc., 1940*), *pp. 274-275. By permission of Mrs. Oscar Ameringer.*

One method for garnering the socialist sheaves was protracted meetings patterned after those of religious congregations. They were held in country schoolhouses, village churches, and more rarely in the courtrooms of county courthouses, and usually lasted a week or two, according to the attendance and the results obtained.

Having selected a promising school district or village, I secured the permission of the proper wardens or directors to use their church or school. Then gathering my little flock together, I started preaching Marxism. As the meeting proceeded, attendance grew so that toward the end there was usually only standing room left, and quite often not even that. In the latter instances, the more faithful would do the standing, or listen to the speaker through the windows from outside. This was done in order to give new converts, or the not yet converted, a chance to hear the message with the least degree of discomfort. What an earnest, self-forgetful bunch those American farmer comrades were!

At every meeting pamphlets were sold, subscriptions and applications for membership taken. On the last night, and as a sort of climax and initiation into the faith, we frequently held box socials. The young ladies of the flock would bring boxes filled with sandwiches, cakes, pies and other delicacies. Then the boxes were auctioned, sight unseen, to the highest bidder. When the young lady was unusually attractive or popular her suitors often bid her box far above its intrinsic value. For box holder and box purchaser were to eat its contents together.

These meetings were usually better than self supporting. Expenses were low: there was no rent to pay; advertising was done by giving "general ring" calls over the party lines, which were free; the speaker was boarded and bedded by one of the comrades. The salary of the preacher was catch as catch can. Speakers and organizers of the Party, as strong advocates of unionism, had organized a union of their own, providing a sliding scale of from twelve to eighteen dollars a week. As one of the stars, I received the top. Any money left over the union scale went to the cause.

Small pay. Plenty of inconvenience and hard work. But please don't waste any sympathy on world savers. Their reward is the joy they get out of saving the world, even if the world stubbornly declines to be saved.

3

J. B. Webster, "A Farmer's Criticism of the Socialist Party"

From The International Socialist Review, *II* (*May 1902*), 769-773.

. . . Whether or not the Socialist Party shall gain definite and lasting headway in the confusion of ideas prevailing at present, depends absolutely upon the policies it may outline in its platform. I have read largely of Socialist literature within the last four years, endeavoring to do so without partisan bias, and from such reading, and a critical examination of the "Immediate Demands" and resolutions on Socialism and Trades Unionism, I am of the opinion that there is no reasonable hope of any considerable affiliation of farmers and other conservative elements of the country with the Socialist movement with its present policies and declarations. . . .

While [trade unions] are important and exercise large political influence because of their concentrated power, nevertheless, in my opinion they will utterly fail of success in gaining control of either state or nation, on the basis of the demands and resolutions referred to, because of the maintenance of the central idea that Trade Unionists and Socialists constitute all there is of humanity worth preserving. If through any political upheaval, amounting to a social revolution, against the tyranny imposed on the masses by plutocracy, the Socialist Party should gain the ascendancy, with its present program, the party would speedily perish in the ruts of its own digging. No party or doctrine can long endure that is not equitable and just in the sight of man, conceding to every human being the rights and immunities claimed by itself. . . . As a farmer of forty years standing, it seems to me that the Socialist Party, with its present policies, offers us no remedy for the grievances of which we complain. . . .

Then, again, it is declared in the resolution on Trades Unionism, that "The exploitation of labor will only come to an end when society takes possession of all the means of production for the benefit of all the people. It is the duty of every trades-unionist to realize the necessity of independent political action on Socialist lines, to join the Socialist Party and assist in building up a strong political movement of the wage-working class, whose ultimate aim and object must be the abolition of wage-slavery and the establishment of a cooperative state of society, based on the collective ownership of all the means of production and distribution."

Here is Bellamyism pure and simple: that the government shall own all property, land and the products of labor, and all the people of the nation shall be its employees, absolutely subject to the will and directions of a central government.

The first objection I have to such an arrangement is that a central power in possession of all the means of production is absolute master of the direction and destiny of the people, and once possessed of such power such a government inevitably becomes an irresponsible despotism, holding its citizens in subjection by the iron hand that always follows concentrated power.

Secondly: I object to this plan of government, because it inevitably destroys all independence of individual action and love of country, for there can be no patriotism in any country where there are no homes founded upon title deeds. Socialism may grow in the countries of Europe, where on the average not one man in fifty owns a foot of land. Tenantry is hereditary and the conception of anything better is foreign to the common mind, and it seems that the highest conception of civilization and independence yet reached in those countries is the changing of the system of serfdom at present prevailing from individual landlordism to that of a government control of all the means of production. But in this country the love of title deeds to homes is inbred among the people. . . .

If the Socialist Party will leave off its extreme views and adopt a platform of principles seemingly tangible and intelligible to the ordinary understanding, there will be a prospect of all the toilers of the nation, in whatever calling engaged, joining its ranks and working for the party's success.

It seems to me that a majority of the farmers of the nation would accept and support a platform of principles taken almost wholly from the Socialist Party "demands," as follows:

a. The Public ownership of all means of transportation and communication and all other public utilities, as well as of all industries controlled by monopolies, trusts, and combines.

b. A graduated income tax.

c. A graduated land tax.

d. The inauguration of a system of public industries, public credit to be used for that purpose in order that the workers be secured the full product of their labor.

e. The education of all children up to the age of 18 years, and State and municipal aid for books, clothing, and food.

f. Equal civil and political rights for men and women.

g. The initiative and referendum, proportional representation, and the right of recall of representatives by their constituents.

h. State or National insurance of working people in case of accidents, lack of employment, sickness and want in old age.

On these propositions the conservative elements of the nation are substantially agreed, including a majority of the farmers. . . .

SOCIALISM AND THE YOUNG INTELLECTUALS

Socialism often appealed to the college youth of the pre-1914 years. It combined a rational approach to social problems with nonconformity. It had a vitality not apparent to many young people in the older parties. Filled with youth's confidence and intrigued by new ideas, they saw no reason to doubt socialism's growth. The cause was something to which they could give themselves.

In September, 1905, Upton Sinclair, already famous as a crusading muckraker and social critic, planned a young people's division of the party. He and others, including some wealthy "parlor pinks," as radical socialists sneered, formed the Inter-Collegiate Socialist Society. It grew rather rapidly, and by 1913 had its own publications, with branches in many famous universities. Since many college students of that period came from middle and upper class backgrounds, the movement seemed illogical, but prospered better than its founders hoped. It had chapters in northeastern schools, in some state universities in the South and Midwest, and in some Protestant denominational schools. Its strongest chapter was, predictably, at Columbia University.

Its propaganda was perhaps more effective than much of its content. In 1905 and 1906, Jack London, a charter member, toured for the ISS in a remarkable display of socialist intellectuality. Dressed in a kind of Little Lord Fauntleroy sailor suit and attended by a Korean valet, London was an astonishing spectacle as well as a major drawing card. He and other red or pink intellectuals wrote and spoke a great deal for socialism.

The party also helped support the Rand School of Social Science, established in 1906, to provide a kind of radical education for the poor in New York City. It helped pay the bills for a Lyceum Bureau that sent speakers and written material to many parts of the country. These efforts to win the intellectual and the youth in American socialism's golden age may now seem unrealistic or naive. But they show what a varied and rich movement it was, and how much it tried to capitalize on America's mental wealth as well as her material discontent.

1

Evans Clark, "The Young Alumni and the I.S.S."

The following is typical of the propaganda "calls" that went out from time to time to organizers and sympathizers among young people. From the Inter-Collegiate Socialist Review, *V, no. 3 (February-March 1917), 20-21.*

I want to urge all of you men and women to carry the I.S.S. out of college with you when you leave and to establish in your home city or town an alumni chapter.

During the few years I have been out of college I have been impressed with the great difference in function between the undergraduate and the alumni chapter. The college chapter serves to introduce the student to Socialism. But the function of the alumni chapter is not that. It is more a matter of making the acquaintanceship mean something in the life of the young graduate. In my opinion this acquaintanceship, if it is to mean anything, demands the fulfillment of some very specific needs.

First of all, there is the necessity that comes to all of us, and especially to college alumni who are Socialists, for human companionship. I think I speak for most of us who have come out of college branded as radicals when I say that we have gone back to our old circle of family and friends to find that the circle has developed many unexpected breaks. Many of our friends have drifted away. We have been considered queer. And on our part we have found that we had few points of contact with those with whom in earlier days we had many. Here, then, is the first real need which an alumni chapter can fill. It can create for us a new circle of friends —friends with whom we can be ourselves with sincerity and frankness, and find response. It can, in a word, furnish us sociability.

Then, too, the wisest young graduates are those who feel in the commencement platform that their education has just begun. And here again is a need which an alumni chapter can meet. By means of meetings at which men and women speak who are doing things in the labor and Socialist ranks the alumni can broaden and deepen their knowledge of the world. An alumni chapter can furnish education.

Lastly, and I think of the greatest importance today, is a need that cries most insistently for satisfaction—the desire to do and to do effectively. I am continually overwhelmed by the disorganization and ineffectiveness of the radical forces in matters of practical politics and affairs. Here again is the opportunity for the alumni chapter. It can furnish a nucleus and stimulus for other organizations, for raising funds for strikers, for securing publicity for some battle of labor, for exposing some crying industrial abuse, for presenting expert testimony before some legislative investigating committee, for a thousand and one skirmishes in the battle on things as they are. An alumni chapter can be an incubator to hatch out plots in the struggle for human emancipation.

I urge you, one and all, then, to organize alumni chapters when you leave college: first in the name of sociability; second, in the name of education and lastly in the name of liberty itself.

2

"The National Socialist Lyceum Lecture Bureau"

From The International Socialist Review, *XII (April 1912), 666-667.*

The report [on a special national lecture program] of the National Lyceum Bureau indicates that it has accomplished one of the greatest pieces of propaganda work ever undertaken by the Socialist Party. In all 1,560 lectures were conducted by 312 locals. The average attendance being over 300, there was in all an attendance of 500,000 up to March 1. The total receipts were $61,-827.62. This means just that amount of subscriptions to papers and books. The distribution of over 2,000,000 pieces of advertising had in itself incalculable propaganda value. It is almost impossible to exaggerate the advantage which organized, systematized lecture courses have over the casual public meetings which most locals have been in the habit of conducting during the winter season. The division of the subject of Socialism into five parts and the discussion of each phase by a competent lecturer was a most fortunate conception. . . . The purpose of the Lecture Course was first, to educate party members and sympathizers in Socialism. Second, to bring new members into the party. Third, to increase the circulation of all legitimate party publications and distribute sound literature. Fourth, and by no means the least important, to get the party membership into the habit of performing propaganda and educational work during the winter time. The Lyceum Bureau has been successful in attaining every one of the purposes with which it set out. Of course there was a considerable number of failures among the weak locals. Nor did the smallest locals prove to be the weakest. What an inspiration it is to find one like that at Plaza, North Dakota, successfully conducting a course to a conclusion. Plaza has but 500 people but its Socialist Local there sold 344 tickets. Many of the Lyceum tickets were sold to surrounding country people and some of them rode as far as thirty miles with the temperature way below zero to attend the lectures. Washington,

Pennsylvania, with a population of 18,000 had an average attendance of 600 and upon the completion of the first course it applied for a second. So many locals made a splendid success of their work that it would be impossible to mention them all.

It might almost be considered strange that we have waited until this late date [1912] before organizing this lecture work. It needs no argument to show that an average local simply cannot secure by itself the speakers needed for a systematic course. And whatever causes in the past may have led some of the state organizations to take a doubtful view of the work of the National Office, these ought not at present to count against the work of the Lyceum Bureau. The far-reaching results of the Bureau's work are much too valuable to permit its discontinuance or weakening by any lesser considerations whatsoever. . . .

It is to be hoped that next year the Lecture Course will be conducted by at least twice as many locals as this year. Intense interest in Socialism everywhere abounds and purely propaganda work is being conducted to a gratifying degree with inspiring enthusiasm. It is the soldier work of education which our American movement has hitherto lacked and which will make it a hundredfold more efficient in the near future. . . .

VI

Socialism in the Age of Normalcy

THE AMERICAN SOCIALISTS BITTERLY AND MILITANTLY OPPOSED intervention in World War I. When the conflict began in Europe in the summer of 1914, they counselled their European brethren to oppose it; when the European socialists voted war credits and sustained the slaughter, the American movement felt a slight chill. Perhaps old-fashioned national patriotism would triumph over internationalism and the socialist dream; and perhaps that triumph would seal socialism's doom.

America entered the conflict on the Allied side in 1917. Meeting in an emergency convention in St. Louis, the socialist party denounced the move and declared its pacifism. But the war strained socialism's precarious unity, and many prominent party members left to join the war effort. The total mobilization of public opinion as well as resources, the strong edge of blind idealism on the sword of war, America's naivete as it entered its first major foreign war, all worked against socialism's pacific stand. To the socialists, the war was merely capitalism's bitter fruit, a conflict provoked by the master class to make money from the blood of the masses.

The conflict ended the spirit of progressive reform among the American people, and brought persecution to all groups opposed to war. The socialists suffered from private community as well as governmental persecution. Freedom of speech and press evaporated, and the party and its affiliates lived in a police state atmosphere. Debs went to prison for violating the Espionage Act in 1918, and remained there until Christmas Day, 1921. He emerged old and broken physically, but as vocally militant as ever.

The Russian revolutions of 1917 compounded the confusion, and with the war's persecution sounded the death knell of

93

American socialism's golden age. By 1919, the party fell into its component parts, and some of its younger members fled into the emerging Communist Party. The conservative socialist leaders like Victor Berger and Morris Hillquit, unwilling to risk the party's total destruction by allying it with Bolshevism, purged the radical elements. By 1920, the socialist party was a shadow of its former self, its press bankrupt, its leaders silenced or jailed, its membership decimated.

Almost all American socialists at first welcomed the revolutions in Russia, for they seemed to fulfill the socialist belief in capitalism's fall, the rising of the workers, and the viciousness of the war. But Bolshevism's growing emphasis on terror and the emergence of a police state turned most American socialists from it. Russian communist leaders' assumption of leadership of the international socialist movement, complete with party discipline and dogmatizing from Moscow, angered old-line American socialists. The American party was never affiliated with communism, and bitterly opposed communist growth. The World War and its aftermath took much of the heart and voice from American socialism. The militant youth went generally to communism; the language federations disappeared; money dried up; many more people were simply bitter at the fiasco and the failure of their dreams, and drifted away. By the early 1920's the party remained in the hands of older men. It continued to print literature, held occasional meetings, ran a few candidates for office, but it looked anachronistic in the Age of Normalcy.

The prosperity of the 1920's seemed to refute the socialist prediction that capitalism was bankrupt. The American socialists fought in vain against the public delusion that prosperity was sound and permanent. The party leadership was moribund until Norman Thomas became prominent late in the decade. There were few good people left to staff the middle and lower ranks.

But the party kept up a brave front. It had pockets of strength in Milwaukee, Seattle, and other cities. Its national office still sent material across the country. Until his death in 1926, Debs did his best to hold the party together at the top. Though its tireless predictions of capitalism's collapse seemed unreal, the party's future was not altogether bleak. By 1930, at the end of the Jazz Age,

Americans knew that something was wrong. Maybe the socialist calamity howlers had been right after all.

1

"Manifesto of the Socialist Party"

The following document offers a fascinating glimpse into the socialist mentality in its interpretation of the causes and results of World War I, its analysis of the ferment of the immediate post-war period, and in its hopes for the future of international socialism. From The American Labor Yearbook, 1919-1920 *(New York: The Rand School of Social Science, 1920), pp. 411-414.*

The capitalist class is now making its last stand in history. It was entrusted with the government of the world. It is responsible for the prevailing chaos. The events of recent years have conclusively demonstrated that capitalism is bankrupt. It has become a dangerous impediment to progress and human welfare. The working class alone has the power to redeem and to save the world.

In every modern country, whether monarchical or republican in form, the capitalist class was in control, monopolized the national wealth and directed the industrial processes.

Its rule has been one of oppression, disorder and civil and international strife.

The capitalist interests of every leading nation fully exploited the resources of their countries, and reduced their peoples to wretchedness and then set out to conquer the markets of the world for the sale of their surplus commodities, for the investment of their surplus capital, and for the acquisition of additional sources of raw material and natural wealth. . . .

The great rival powers of the world were uneasily and distrustfully watching each other and arming against each other. . . . Capitalism in its full development caused human society to revert to the primitive conditions of savage tribal warfare.

Then came the inevitable collapse. The world was precipitated into the most savage and inhuman slaughter in history. . . .

Finally the ghastly combat ended. The Central Powers, vanquished and exhausted, laid down their arms. Imperialistic statesmen of the victorious allies dictated a so-called peace. It is a peace of hatred and violence, a peace of vengeance and strangulation. The reactionary statesmen at the Versailles peace conference were blinded by greed, passion, and fear. They refused to heed the terrible lesson of the great war. They have left open the old international sores and have inflicted innumerable and grievous new wounds upon a distracted world.

To strengthen their precarious rule of violence and reaction the triumphant representatives of Allied capitalism have created an Executive Committee of their governments, which they have the insolence to parade under the counterfeit label of a League of Nations. . . .

In the United States, Capitalism has emerged from the war more reactionary and aggressive, more insolent and oppressive than it has ever been.

Having entered the war "to make the world safe for democracy," our government has enthusiastically allied itself with the most reactionary imperialism of Europe and Asia. . . .

And while thus serving as an accomplice of black reaction abroad, our administration and the capitalist interests behind it were busily engaged in the ruthless work of suppressing civil rights and liberties at home.

Under the pretext of wartime necessity, Congress and state legislatures enacted drastic laws, which effectively nullified the right of political criticism and opposition, freedom of speech, of the press, and of assemblage. . . . The Socialist Party, which during the war was the only party of peace and progress and the sole political defender of civil rights and labor's interests in the United States, was brutally outlawed. Its press was crippled, many of its meetings were dispersed, a great number of its defenders were persecuted and jailed. . . .

It is not surprising, therefore, that the end of the war has found the organized workers far behind their brothers in Europe who are everywhere strengthening their forces to throw off the chains of industrial and political subjugation.

But even in the United States the symptoms of a rebellious spirit in the ranks of the working masses are daily multiplying. The widespread and extensive strikes for better labor conditions, the demand of the two million railway workers to control their industry, the sporadic formation of labor parties apparently though not fundamentally in opposition to the political parties of the possessing class, are promising indications of a definite tendency on the part of American labor to break away from its reactionary and futile leadership and to join in the great emancipating movement of the more advanced revolutionary workers of the world. . . .

The people of Russia, like the American colonists in 1776, were driven by their rulers to the use of violent methods to secure and maintain their freedom. The Socialist Party calls upon the workers of the United States to do all in their power to restore and maintain our civil rights to the end that the transition from capitalism to Socialism may be effected without resort to the drastic measures made necessary by autocratic despotism.

We are utterly opposed to the so-called League of Nations. Against this international alliance of capitalist governments, we hold out to the world the ideal of a federation of free and equal Socialist nations. . . .

The great purpose of the Socialist Party is to wrest the industries and the control of the government of the United States from the capitalists and their retainers. It is our purpose to place industry and government in the control of the workers with hand and brain, to be administered for the benefit of the whole community.

To insure the triumph of Socialism in the United States the bulk of the American workers must be strongly organized politically as Socialists, in constant, clear-cut and aggressive opposition to all parties of the possessing class. They must be strongly organized on the economic field on broadly industrial lines, as one powerful and harmonious class organization, cooperating with the Socialist Party, and ready in cases of emergency to reinforce the political demands of the working class by industrial action.

To win the American workers from their ineffective and demoralizing leadership, to educate them to an enlightened understanding of their own class interests, and to train and assist them to organize politically and industrially on class lines in order to effect their emancipation,—that is the supreme task confronting the Socialist Party of America.

To this great task, without deviation or compromise, we pledge all our energies and resources. For its accomplishment we call for the support and cooperation of the workers of America and of all other persons desirous of ending the insane rule of capitalism before it has had the opportunity to precipitate humanity into another cataclysm of blood and ruin.

Long live the international Socialist revolution, the only hope of the suffering world!

2

David Karsner, "The Passing of the Socialist Party"

Karsner, Debs' biographer and a prominent younger socialist sympathizer before and during World War I, found the 1920's deeply disillusioning. In this article he shrewdly analyzes the reasons for socialism's decline after the war, and for its failure to take root in America. From Current History, *XX (June 1924), 402-407. © by Current History, Inc. Reprinted by permission of Current History, Inc.*

After twenty-three years of indifferent gains and losses, the Socialist Party goes into eclipse with the presidential campaign of 1924. There is scarcely enough of it left to salvage and weld with another group. It has neither good will nor bad to bequeath to another organization. It is a political ghost stalking in the graveyard of current events seeking respectable burial. The majority of its former voting membership is back in the Democratic and Republican Parties from which it came. Its foreign membership seceded five years ago, affiliating with Communist groups. . . . In truth there is no radical movement in America worthy of first-class notice, and none knows this better than the radical body itself. . . .

The factors which contributed to the debacle of the Socialist Party were the World War, the Russian Bolshevist revolution, and the imprisonment of Debs in Atlanta Penitentiary for nearly three years as a consequence of his disapproval of American participation in the war. Residing deep in these factors, however, was utter confusion of Socialists in their attitude toward American issues and psychology. They possessed the crusader's impatience of the technologist. Blinded by the illusory panorama of the Pleasant Pastures toward which they were headed, they tried to ignore and evade the stubbles of material fact and psychological inference that tripped and ensnared them. . . .

The Socialists seek to achieve their program for social and economic change through political action, and this medium is controlled by social and economic forces that do not desire a departure from the present social order. The Socialist Party, therefore, is hamstrung in its ultimate aims, and its immediate demands may be realized more quickly by mass pressure upon either the Democratic or Republican Party. . . .

In cities where Socialists have been elected to office, local issues have been stressed, and the major program has remained an interesting thesis for students of political economy and the Department of Justice. Our government can be frightened into any political expediency or economic inanity when sufficient pressure is brought to bear upon the major political parties. Prohibition is a striking example of this. Woman suffrage was first advocated and avowed as a political issue by the Socialist Party, but the Nineteenth Amendment was a victory for a class of people who were not Socialists and who would disclaim any affinity with socialism. . . .

The World War proved that Socialists are victims of the same emotions and prejudices that ensnare us all. Historically committed against war and preparation for it, Socialists divided on those issues in every country in the world where they maintained any semblance of organization. . . . In the American Congress, Meyer London of New York, the sole [socialist] member, voted against American participation in the war, but he voted for several military measures for its prosecution, excepting the Espionage law. The day before America declared war against Germany the Socialists held a convention in St. Louis and adopted a resolution proclaiming not only their disapproval of all war but their opposition to this one in particular, and the resolution said something about "mass demonstrations" to put it down. . . .

Despite previous declarations of conscientious objection, thousands of Socialists donned the khaki. Morris Hillquit, Socialist candidate for mayor in New York in 1917, polled approximately 145,000 votes, but it was admitted even by Socialists that this total was inflated by pro-German and pacifist ballots. . . .

In 1919 there were nearly 120,000 dues-paying members of the Socialist Party. In May, 1923, the Socialist Convention in New York was told that the membership had dropped to 12,474. Eighty delegates attended that convention while 281 delegates gathered at the Indianapolis convention in 1912. In the latter year Debs . . . polled 897,011 votes, doubling his total of 1908. In 1916 with the war in Europe and with American political and industrial issues brought sharply to the front, Allan Benson was able to muster only 585,113 votes. Four years later, with universal suffrage, Debs, then a war prisoner at Atlanta, polled 919,799 votes . . .

In 1912 there were seventy Socialist papers published in English in the United States, and thirty-one in foreign languages. In 1923 there were not more than twenty Socialist weeklies published in English and a dozen in foreign languages. This excludes the trade union and Communist weeklies, which Socialists have always ignored except to attack and deride. In 1923 the Socialists were obliged to sell their building in Chicago, where they maintained a national headquarters, and to move to a loft of modest capacity. In 1912 one hundred persons were on the payroll of the national office. In 1923 this number had been reduced to five. . . .

The Socialist program is preposterous when read from the standpoint of its ultimate objectives. It promises what it cannot deliver, human nature being what it is. It is neither good nor wise to promise man more than may be given him. Kings have lost their heads by that folly, and the cemeteries of civilization are strewn with the ashes of empires that promised much and yielded little. The Church has been wise in telling people that their reward awaited them in heaven. The Socialists and other radical groups, however, reject the idea of deferring the journey of the Upward Way until death cures them of want. They say that the golden dawn is possible here and now, and they assert it so persistently that millions, especially the suffering and struggling poor, have enlisted in the armies of

Human Betterment and trodden the darksome paths toward Utopia.

Many of us, at one time and another, have joined this or that group with the hope of improving ourselves in some manner. How many, however, realize, as they take the Upward Way, that they are only setting forth on the same track that has attracted others at different times through all the ages, and that the sunlit corridors, or the darksome passages that bid us on, are adorned with the achievements or scarred with the bloody footprints of those who have trekked that way before and are no more?

Those who give themselves wholly in spirit to these movements, who make no paltry reservations for themselves, are destined to find themselves sooner or later stranded in that heavily populated street of Disillusion. They find, as they march in the armies of redemption, that their fellows are not divine, because they are human; that the Cause and the Crusader may indeed have very little in common; that prejudice, selfishness, malevolent purpose, envy and false witness are not infrequently the drum corps to whose martial air the sweetly illusioned ones are obliged to keep step. They may not know this until they commence to question the circuitous route that lies ahead and the ultimate distance between where they are bivouacked and the Pleasant Pastures. . . .

Socialists believe in government by majority. They embrace democracy and woo the will of the people in a lover's lane of political theorizing. Actually, your Socialist is a conformist. He may not conform to present standards, but he would conform to those made for him by his political priests. He is not intellectually free, but is a standardist. He carries in his pocket a chart and a reprint for personal conduct and association. Of recent years I have wondered what would happen to a Savonarola, a Giordano Bruno, a Galileo, an Anatole France, should he stumble into the ranks of the Socialists.

There are social, political, and economic changes which are highly desirable and poignantly necessary. Socialists seem to know better than some other people what some of these changes portend. It seems to me, however, after some ten years of rather intimate journalistic association with their leaders and laymen, that they are wholly without equipment, mentally, ethically, or spiritually, to do more than debate these social problems.

3

"The Socialist Party Platform, 1928"

From The Intelligent Voter's Guide (*New York: Socialist Party, 1928*), *pp. 11-16.*

PUBLIC OWNERSHIP AND CONSERVATION

To recover the rightful heritage of the people we propose:

a. Nationalization of our natural resources, beginning with the coal mines and water sites, particularly at Boulder Dam and Muscle Shoals.

b. A publicly owned giant power system under which the Federal Government shall cooperate with the States and municipalities in the distribution of electrical energy to the people at cost. Only when public agencies have full control over the generation, transmission, and distribution of electrical power can the consumers be guaranteed against exploitation by the great electrical interests of the country. Public ownership of these and other industries must include employee representation in the management, and the principle of collective bargaining must be recognized.

c. National ownership and democratic management of railroads and other means of transportation and communication.

d. An adequate national program for flood control and flood relief, reforestation, irrigation, and reclamation.

UNEMPLOYMENT RELIEF

To relieve the tragic misery of millions of unemployed workers and their families we propose:

a. The immediate governmental relief of the unemployed by extension of all public works and a program of long-range planning of public works following the present depression. All persons thus employed to be engaged at hours and wages fixed by bona fide labor unions.

b. Loans to States and municipalities for the purpose of carrying on public works and the taking of such other measures as will lessen widespread misery.

c. A system of unemployment insurance.

d. The nation-wide extension of public employment agencies in cooperation with city federations of labor.

LABOR LEGISLATION

The lives and well-being of the producers and their families should be the first charge on society. We therefore urge:

a. A system of health and accident insurance and of old-age pensions, as well as unemployment insurance. As long as the workers are dependent primarily upon their employers rather than on the community for protection against the exigencies of old age, sickness, accident, and unemployment, employers hostile or indifferent to the labor movement will be able to use their private insurance schemes as powerful weapons against organized labor.

b. Shortening the work day in keeping with the steadily increasing productivity of labor due to improvements in machinery and methods.

c. Securing to every worker a rest period of no less than two days in each week.

d. Enacting of a Federal anti-child labor amendment.

e. Abolition of the brutal exploitation of convicts under the contract system and substitution of a cooperative organization of industries in penitentiaries and workshops for the benefit of convicts and their dependents, the products to be used in public institutions, and the convict workers to be employed at wages current in the industry.

f. Legislation aiming at the prevention of occupational diseases.

TAXATION

For the proper support of Government and as a step toward social justice we propose:

a. Increase of taxation on high income levels, of corporation taxes and inheritance taxes, the proceeds to be used for old-age pensions and other forms of social insurance.

b. Appropriation by taxation of the annual rental value of all land held for speculation.

CIVIL LIBERTIES

To secure to the people the civil rights without which democracy is impossible we demand:

a. Federal legislation to enforce the first amendment to the Constitution so as to guarantee effectually freedom of speech, press, and assembly, and to penalize any official who interferes with the civil rights of any citizen.

b. Abolition of injunctions in labor disputes.

c. Repeal of the espionage law and of other repressive legislation and restoration of civil and political rights to those unjustly convicted under war-time laws, with reimbursement for time served.

d. Legislation protecting foreign born workers from deportation and from refusal of citizenship on account of political opinions.

e. Modification of immigration laws to permit the reuniting of families and to offer a refuge for those fleeing from political or religious persecution.

f. Abolition of detective agencies engaged in inter-state business.

ANTI-LYNCHING

As a measure of protection for the oppressed, especially for our Negro fellow citizens, we propose:

a. Enactment of the Berger anti-lynching bill making participation in lynching a felony.

POLITICAL DEMOCRACY

The Constitution of the United States was drafted in 1787 and was designed to meet conditions utterly different from those prevailing today. In order to make our form of government better suited to the exigencies of the times we propose the immediate calling of a constitutional convention.

A modernized Constitution should provide, among other things, for the election of the President and Vice-President by direct popular vote of the people, for reduction of the representation in Congress of those States where large sections of the citizens are disfranchised by force or fraud, for proportional representation, and for the abolition of the usurped power of the Supreme Court to pass upon the constitutionality of legislation enacted by Congress.

CREDIT AND BANKING

For our emancipation from the money trust, we propose:

a. Nationalization of the banking and currency system, beginning with extension of the service of the postal-savings banks to cover every department of the banking business.

FARM RELIEF

The Socialist Party believes that the farmer is entitled to special consideration because of the importance of agriculture, because of the farmer's present economic plight, and because the farmer is unable to control the prices of what he buys and what he sells. Many of the party's demands, including public development of electrical energy, nationalization of coal and railroads, and reform of the credit system, will be of distinct benefit to the farmer.

As a further means of agricultural relief, we propose:

a. Acquisition by bona fide cooperative societies and by Federal, State, and municipal governments of grain elevators, stockyards, storage warehouses, and other distributing agencies and the conduct of these services on a non-profit basis.

b. Encouragement of farmers' cooperative purchasing and marketing societies and of credit agencies.

c. Social insurance against losses due to adverse weather conditions, such as hail, drought, cyclone, and flood.

INTERNATIONAL RELATIONS

We are unalterably opposed to imperialism and militarism, therefore we propose:

a. Immediate withdrawal of American forces from Nicaragua and abandonment of the policy of military intervention in Central America and other countries.

b. That all private loans and investments of American citizens in foreign countries shall be made at the sole risk of the bondholders and investors. The United States Government shall not resort to any military or other coercive intervention with foreign countries for the protection of such loans and investments.

c. Cancellation of all war debts due the United States from its former associated powers on condition of a simultaneous cancellation of all international debts, and a corresponding remission of the reparation obligations of the Central Powers, and on the further condition that our debtors reduce their military expenditures below pre-war level. The Socialist Party especially denounces the debt-settling policy of our Government in favoring the Facist dictatorship of Italy and thereby helping to perpetuate the political enslavement of the Italian nation.

d. Recognizing both the services and the limitations of the League of Nations—the need of revision of its covenant and of the Treaty of Versailles—we unite with the workers of Europe in demanding that the League be made all inclusive and democratic, and that the machinery for the revision of the peace treaties under article 19 of the covenant be elaborated and made effective. We favor the entry of the United States into the League of Nations at the time and under conditions which will further these causes and promote the peace of the world.

e. The recognition of the Russian Soviet Government.

f. Aggressive activity against militarism, against the large Army and Navy program of our present administration, and in behalf of International Disarmament.

g. Treaties outlawing war and the substitution of peaceful methods for the settlement of international disputes.

h. Independence of the Philippines on terms agreed upon in negotiations with the Filipinos, autonomy for Puerto Rico, and civil government for the Virgin Islands.

VII

American Socialism
and the Great Depression

TERRIBLE AS IT MIGHT SEEM TO THE SENSITIVE PERSON, THE FALLING price indexes, slumping wages, rising unemployment, and public despair of the early 1930's were a kind of godsend to American socialism. Every indicator, rational and emotional, proved to many that the socialists had been right. They said that capitalism after all was irresponsible and brutal. Though appalled at the system's collapse after 1929, the socialists were not exactly grateful. Bread-lines, hungry children, and evicted farmers did not bolster their spirits. Having so long predicted the reckoning, however, they could not afford to avoid meeting it.

Though their numbers dwindled under wartime persecution, fear of international radicalism, and the prosperity of the 1920's, the American socialists were never totally silent. As their support among workers, the middle class, the youth and other groups dwindled after 1917, they gained vocal allegiance among articulate intellectuals. By the time of the Great Depression, though a shadow of its 1912 image, the party had recovered enough strength to seem vital again. It had at least a skeleton press; liberal publications were open to socialist writers; its predictions had proved true. It attracted some support from the discontented and seemed to have everything to gain from capitalism's collapse.

American socialism had produced a national leader to replace the dead Debs, Norman Thomas. His pilgrimage to socialism was typical of the pre-1914 youth. Born in 1884 in Marion, Ohio, the son of a Presbyterian minister, Thomas quickly displayed a love of the written word. He was an avid reader and as his horizons

107

expanded so did his interest in social questions. He attended Princeton University, working part time to help meet expenses, and graduated in 1905. After a world tour and some social work, he entered Union Theological Seminary and graduated in 1911. He was then a Presbyterian minister in an East Harlem neighborhood that impressed upon him all the worst of capitalism's evils. Unlike Debs, his conversion to socialism was slow and rather undramatic. He was a Progressive in 1912 and a Democrat in 1916. His pacifism and sharpened social conscience took him to socialism during the World War, and in the 1920's he emerged as the party's most promising national leader.

Though an intellectual and an eloquent speaker, Thomas had only formal ties with Marxism. Christianity was his wellspring, and he saw no division between its teachings and democratic socialism. He was essentially a planner, but blessed with a magnificent voice, a fine stage presence and a compelling vitality, he was a spellbinding political candidate cut on the Debs model. He appealed, however, to the educated and the intellectual; Debs had appealed to the working masses. Thomas cherished logic and reason; Debs frankly favored emotion. The two men well symbolized their respective socialist parties.

If the American socialists really hoped to capture any political power during the 1930's they were greatly disappointed. In 1932, Thomas polled 884,781 votes; in 1936, after four years of New Deal reform, his tally slumped to 187,342. In true American fashion the people preferred the New Deal reform to outright socialism. But Thomas and his followers were influential, and were tireless in their educational propagandizing. The ideas they put forward indirectly affected the New Deal program.

But party membership lagged behind its vocal leaders; it never rose above 21,000 between 1929 and 1936. As in older days when the air was more exuberant and hopes higher, American socialism relied on its message to educate its hearers. Its political victories seemed small in comparison to its efforts, but who could tell what its campaigns really meant to America in the long run?

1

"A Plan for America: The Socialist Platform of 1932"

A comparison of the party platforms of 1928 and 1932 shows how well socialism's rhetoric and ideas adapted to the Depression. It also shows how similar many of the socialist ideas were to the laws and programs established by the New Deal. From A Plan For America *(Chicago: Socialist Party, 1932), pp. 10-15.*

UNEMPLOYMENT AND LABOR LEGISLATION

a. A federal appropriation of $5,000,000,000 for immediate relief for those in need, to supplement state and local appropriations.

b. A federal appropriation of $5,000,000,000 for public works and roads, reforestation, slum clearance and decent homes for the workers, by federal government, state and cities.

c. Legislation providing for the acquisition of land, buildings and equipment necessary to put the unemployed to work producing food, fuel and clothing and for the erection of houses for their own use.

d. The six-hour day and the five-day week without a reduction of wages.

e. A comprehensive and efficient system of free public employment agencies.

f. A compulsory system of unemployment compensation with adequate benefits, based on contributions by the government and by employers.

g. Old age pensions for men and women sixty years of age and over.

h. Health and maternity insurance.

i. Improved system of workmen's compensation and accident insurance.

j. The abolition of child labor.

k. Government aid to farmers and small home owners to protect them against mortgage foreclosures and a moratorium on sales for non-payment of taxes by destitute farmers and unemployed workers.

l. Adequate minimum wage laws.

SOCIAL OWNERSHIP

a. Public ownership and democratic control of mines, forest, oil, and power resources; public utilities dealing with light and power, transportation and communication, and of all other basic industries.

b. The operation of these publicly owned industries by boards of administration on which the wage-worker, the consumer and the technician are adequately represented; the recognition in each industry of the principles of collective bargaining and civil service.

BANKING

a. Socialization of our credit and currency system and the establishment of a unified banking system, beginning with the complete governmental acquisition of the Federal Reserve Banks and the extension of the services of the Postal Savings Banks to cover all departments of the banking business and the transference of this department of the post office to a government-owned banking corporation.

TAXATION

a. Steeply increased inheritance taxes and income taxes on the higher incomes and estates of both corporations and individuals.

b. A constitutional amendment authorizing the taxation of all governmental securities.

AGRICULTURE

Many of the foregoing measures for socializing the power, banking, and other industries, for raising living standards among the city workers, etc., would greatly benefit the farming population.

As special measures for agricultural upbuilding, we propose:

a. The reduction of tax burdens, by a shift from taxes on farm property to taxes on incomes, inheritances, excess profits, and other similar forms of taxation.

b. Increased federal and state subsidies to road building and education and social services for rural communities.

c. The creation of a federal marketing agency for the purchase and marketing of agricultural products.

d. The acquisition by bona fide cooperative societies and by governmental agencies of grain elevators, stockyards, packing houses and warehouses and the conduct of these services on a non-profit basis. The encouragement of farmers' cooperative societies and of consumers' cooperatives in the cities, with a view of eliminating the middleman.

e. The socialization of federal land banks and the extension by these banks of long-term credit to farmers at low rates of interest.

f. Social insurance against losses due to adverse weather conditions.

g. The creation of national, regional, and state land utilization boards for the purpose of discovering the best uses of the farming land of the country, in view of the joint needs of agriculture, industry, recreation, water supply, reforestation, etc., and to prepare the way for agricultural planning on a national and, ultimately, on a world scale. . . .

Editor's Note: The party's recommendations in 1932 on constitutional changes, civil liberties, and international affairs remained virtually the same as in the platform of 1928.

2

Norman Thomas, "The Issues of the Day"

In his letter of acceptance of the party's presidential nomination in 1932, Thomas displayed the force, smooth style, and logic that commended him on the platform and by which he made socialism's message the more appealing in the great crisis of the early 1930's. From A Plan For America (*Chicago: Socialist Party, 1932*), *pp. 27-31.*

. . . This presidential campaign falls in a year of crisis. Before our eyes the Socialist prediction of the breakdown of capitalism is being fulfilled with a rapidity and completeness that even the most convinced Socialist in 1928 scarcely expected to see in America. In less than four years from the time our gambler's civilization was at the height of its boasted but tinsel prosperity this collapse has come. . . .

What did the old parties do?

The Republican convention of place holders obediently if un-enthusiastically endorsed Hoover and all his works. Their vague, wordy, indecisive platform is a perfect example of what happens when a political party is obliged to face facts that its outworn theory of rugged individualism cannot account for. The platform is de-signed to get votes from the fear-ridden workers whose interests are by no means the interests of big business which owns the Republican party and exploits the masses. Hoover, prophet of no government in business, has done nothing at all through his ad-ministration but put the government in business, almost always badly, and always in the service of private profit. What he has not done for the unemployed or permitted to be done constitutes a tragedy of the first magnitude for millions of his fellow cit-izens. . . .

If one interprets the Democratic platform in the light of Dem-ocratic performance in the Democratic South where social legisla-tion is at least a generation behind the times, where Negro workers can't vote at all and white workers only if they pay a poll tax; or in Democratic performance in the corrupt machine-ruled Democratic cities of the North like New York or Jersey City; or, most striking of all, of the Democratic record in Congress in the matter of tariffs, sales taxes, unemployment relief, and every vital issue, the mockery of offering anything Democratic as truly progressive becomes even more evident.

It's the old story. Many so-called progressives are getting ready once more to throw away their votes by trying to be "practical" and choose the lesser of two evils. They childishly think they can make progress by voting *against* something they don't like. Wall Street will not worry much about the progressives so long as the height of progressivism is voting for Roosevelt. . . .

Not the politicians but a crazy, cruel, profit-mad capitalism has brought us to this monstrous tragedy that millions of us starve in the midst of actual or potential plenty. A purely negative disgust at all politics rather than at the capitalist system only helps along the drift to fascism: that is, to a dictatorship essentially capitalistic in nature. Such a drift is more and more pronounced in America where men openly call for "an American Mussolini" and discuss "a super government" and evolve Swope plans for capitalist syndicalism with a few sops to keep the workers quiet. Fascism is disaster and can avert [the] catastrophe of a new world war only for a short time, if at all.

The one reasonable alternative to Fascism is Socialism. Whatever its intentions American Communism, by its talk of inevitable violence and ruthless dictatorship, and its tactics of lies and slander against Socialists and trade unionists who do not agree with it, plays into the hands of Fascism. . . .

Socialism in America seeks not to destroy democracy but to fulfill it. International Socialism, we believe, is the alternative to the unimaginable disaster of a new world war rather than its consequence. It will be the final answer to economic insecurity and the ultimate victory over the dark realms of poverty. . . .

Socialism offers the only sound principle of action. The wonder is not that we fare so badly but that we are no worse off when in an interdependent world we own and manage things necessary for our common life, not collectively for the use of all, but privately and for the profit of an owning class. We proclaim hope. No longer do we need to foretell the doom of capitalism. Already men are caught in the fear, insecurity, and poverty that foretell the end. Our business is to show the reasonableness of the Socialist philosophy and the excellence of the Socialist proposal to transfer to public ownership and to democratic management, for use and not for profit, the principal means of production and distribution, the system of banking and credit, and the great natural resources.

We offer not only the one true hope for reorganizing our economic life but also immediate plans for making things better. We are aware that masses of men will not vote for deeper purgatory now in the dubious hope of paradise hereafter. Hence we are concerned with programs to keep the peace *now,* to relieve unemployment *now*, to help the farmers *now*. We ask you to examine our platform from this point of view. Are not our demands "practical" as no other proposals are; practical, that is, for all those who are not trying above all things to hang onto the wealth and power which a comparatively small owning class controls? . . .

3

Norman Thomas to Gabriel Heatter, "The Future of the Socialist Party"

After the election of 1932, prominent newsman and radio commentator Gabriel Heatter, challenged Thomas to prove that socialism had a future in America. Thomas' reply is reprinted from The Nation, *CXXXV (December 14, 1932), 584-586.*

. . . Mr. Heatter's open letter is a good statement of the familiar cry for a new name and less dogmatism in Socialist tactics. (He might be surprised to learn how much less of this sort of criticism there is proportionately than in former years.) Probably the most effective use I can make of the space *The Nation* has put at my disposal is not to answer Mr. Heatter in detail but to discuss affirmatively the situation in which not only the Socialist Party but all thoughtful men who are disquieted by the status quo find themselves as the result of the recent anti-Hoover stampede.

The Socialist vote that was counted—and I have a steadily accumulating body of evidence that, as usual, a large part of it was not counted—will be considerably more than three times that of 1928. It was, however, only about half of what conservative observers expected as a result of the size of our meetings—which, by the way, were predominantly working class—the indications of straw votes, and the general volume of publicity we received. . . . I have learned by definite reports from more than one State that as a matter of fact many of those who voted Socialist in the straw ballot switched at the last moment to Roosevelt in a panic lest Hoover might win. Such shortsighted panic is not a peculiarity of manual workers. It is a general American political phenomenon, not the less disquieting for that reason to those of us who want to make political action useful in times when revolutionary change is demanded. The American electorate has proved in the last two elections that it is capable of ignoring traditional party allegiance, but it does this as yet only to express its fears or hates. It is incredible that an intelligent electorate with any real faith in the positive values of political action should act so negatively. This deep-seated and disquieting malady among our people could hardly be reached by a mere change in the Socialist name.

Look at the facts. This is the worst depression in American history. Fear and discontent are almost universal. Certainly they are universal among the masses of workers and farmers. Almost as widespread as the discontent is a cynical disbelief in both of the old parties and in politicians in general. The amount of talk of the probable necessity for violent action in some vague future would amaze the observer who judges America wholly by election returns. . . .

Did [the] collapse of minor parties [such as the Communist Party] mean that, as in 1896, their ideas had captured one of the major parties? By no means. Never in a time of depression did the principal candidate of the outs offer so little as Governor Roosevelt. He won. Progressives come very cheap in modern America. All that they wanted to know this year was that Governor Roosevelt was not President Hoover. They put cotton in their ears and blinders on their eyes to keep from knowing his record or his program. He was able with impunity to spend the last two or three weeks of his campaign in a satisfactory demonstration to Wall Street that he was entirely safe. . . .

Against this the St. Louis *Post-Dispatch* editorially advances the argument that weak as the Socialist Party is, Socialist measures are always winning because the party, or life itself, somehow manages to force them on one or both of the old parties. There is much truth in that statement, but these indirect gains of socialism are achieved too partially and too late to be of great service to a people swept on toward the downfall of a social order.

The moral of this story is certainly more than the failure of the Socialist name to appeal to the American people. Indeed, on the positive side, if space permitted, I could quote conversations and letters in support of the statement that this year socialism as socialism commanded new and widespread interest and aroused little of the old antagonism. Voters in Milwaukee, Reading, Bridgeport, and New York are little terrified of a name in voting for municipal candidates. . . .

Remember that we have not anything like as many years for slow change as it seemed in 1924 that we should have. If we are to escape catastrophe or a fascism which is in itself disaster we must get intelligent and effective action both at home and abroad in a very few years. There are no signs whatever of any such degree of automatic economic recovery as would give capitalism any marked reprieve through a return of prosperity. The situation demands planning. But purpose must precede plan. Neither manual nor white-collar workers can be aroused and united by a mere pragmatic program. . . .

I do not believe that the mass of workers will continue to ignore our program. The predestined failure of the Democratic Party with its amazingly incompatible elements North and South, East and West; the certainty that out of Mr. Roosevelt's vaulting ambition and shrewd political sense no adequate statesmanship can be born—witness his stand in the matter of foreign debts—give us high hope that the interest in socialism already expressed in America may be carried into action. . . .

I did not say [any of] this in any spirit of recrimination. The crisis before us is too vast for that. It is a crisis which forces us to face two questions: First, do the philosophy and the program of socialism show us the way out? Second, if so, how can we best organize to make that philosophy and program effective? How shall we arouse the solidarity of a working class which so far has failed to assert that solidarity even in a time of crisis? Believing as I do that socialism and only socialism is the hope of the world, I am solely concerned with the second question, and I am very little interested in those who would tell me that we might win greater seeming success at the price of sacrificing the philosophy and program in which alone is hope. On the contrary, the supreme necessity for those of us who would escape dictatorship and catastrophic violence is a new birth of intelligent audacity in the Socialist appeal and the Socialist organization the world over.

4

Norman Thomas, "Surveying the New Deal"

Two years later, with the first phase of the New Deal program enacted and operating, and with the economy rising slowly, Thomas surveyed what the Democrats had done. From The World Tomorrow, *XVII (January 18, 1934), 37-38.*

. . . First, let us review the agricultural situation. It cannot be said that the farming states are happy or will stop the cry for something more: inflation, or a guaranteed price in excess of the cost of production. Enough money, however, is coming from the Federal government into corn, wheat, and cotton states to make them feel a little better. This subsidization of economic scarcity isn't going to work economically very long. The reduction in crops is not going to equal the reduction in acreage. Next year we may, by intensive cultivation, get as much or more than on the old acreage. . . . Fundamental farm problems are still untouched. I refer to landlordism, taxation, debt, and marketing. . . . Farmers seem to be a bit suspicious of both of two rather contradictory policies of the Federal government: (a) the policy of settling the unemployed, or some of them, on subsistence farms; and (b) the policy of displacing farmers by buying submarginal land to put back into forests—in itself a good thing, if the farmers can be taken care of.

Secretary [of Agriculture Henry A.] Wallace, wiser than the present law, sees the need of thinking in terms of world hunger and modifying our trade policies accordingly. But once we have started subsidizing everybody—manufacturers by tariffs, farmers by the processing tax—it will be hard to change things even for the ultimate good of the subsidized. Clearly the New Deal has only temporized with agricultural chaos and distress.

The next aspect to be considered is the National Recovery Administration. This feature of the New Deal, originally adopted not purely out of social realism, but to stop the compulsory thirty-hour week proposed by Senator Black, after some at least seeming success in social reform is working out very unsatisfactorily. It is rapidly losing the confidence of workers. General [Hugh S.] Johnson is a good ballyhoo artist, but he is either so definitely on the employers' side or so weak that he has "cracked down" on nobody with any real strength. November saw a decline in employment of more than 300,000, according to A.F. of L. figures. Few codes provide the 35-hour week in dead earnest and some permit the 54-hour week. The NRA has no central plan. Its chief economic advisor today is a man borrowed from General Motors! . . . the NRA has not so much changed the distribution of the national income as between owners and workers as it has changed it between classes and workers. It is not wholly, but all too largely, a glorified form of work sharing.

The third point is unemployment relief. It is part of Mr. Roosevelt's strength that he manages to be one jump ahead of each crisis. The thing that has saved him and the country from riots and the unemployed from starvation is the Civil Works Administration. Relief funds were running out, public works weren't filling the bill, when the President started the C.W.A. under the able direction of Harry Hopkins. It is probably the chief source of the President's continued popularity among the workers. It is better than the old relief system, and considerable skill has been shown in finding worthwhile jobs in contrast with the jobs that relief agencies had been handing out. The C.W.A., or some substitute for it—perhaps social insurance?—will have to be far more permanent than the President contemplates in his budget message. You can't take away work and other relief from the unemployed without trouble. . . .

Fourth, there is the problem presented by the mounting debt. The immense figures the President gave us in his budget message confirms what I have previously written about the necessity for tackling this terrific burden. A seven billion dollar deficit in a single year invites drastic inflation or deflation, with ruin either way. I repeat what I have already written: the remedy for a staggering load of debt is a capital levy. The financing of debt and the reform of money, banking and credit require a socialized banking system. It ought not to be necessary to add to the natural wealth through public works only at the price of adding an immense burden of interest or indebtedness. With safeguards it ought to be possible to pay for public works especially those which can be made actually or approximately self-liquidating, by non-interest bearing treasury notes—money secured by the public works themselves. Of course such notes will go into general circulation and give us a new kind of money, but a kind as well secured as any in a nation off the gold standard—a standard which is itself of dubious security, as we have learned, in time of trouble. These notes will primarily be directed to those most in need—the unemployed; and they will add to production as they add to money, thus differing from fiat money, which represents no increase in production. Surely this proposal should not be thrown out the window as unorthodox, without examination. . . . Meanwhile, no sensible man can shut his eyes to this debt burden and to the capital levy and simply shout: "Sound Money!" Neither can anyone balance the extraordinary budget by depriving the unemployed of C.W.A assistance or of relief, and letting them starve.

This partial review of the New Deal . . . shows that behind superficial criticism is the fundamental fact that we live in a disintegrating capitalism. You can't prime the capitalist pump, because it is rapidly wearing out. Socialization and planned production for use, not a reformist stabilization or attempted stabilization of capitalism, is the solution.

5

"The Socialist Platform, 1936"

From Porter and Johnson, American Party Platforms 1840-1956 *(Urbana, Illinois: University of Illinois Press, 1956), pp. 370-372. Copyright © 1956 by the University of Illinois Press. Reprinted by permission of the University of Illinois Press.*

. . . Eight years ago the people of this country voted to continue the capitalist Old Deal. The purpose of this deal was to preserve the rights of the few who own most of the Nation's wealth. Under the Old Deal the economic machine was plunged into the worst depression in our history.

Four years ago the voters of the United States threw their support to the New Deal. They elected to office Franklin D. Roosevelt and the Democratic Party. The New Deal, like the Old Deal, has utterly failed. Under it big business was given almost unheard-of powers. Untold wealth was destroyed. Prices rose. Profits advanced. Wages lagged. Twelve million men and women are still jobless, and hunger and destitution exist throughout the land.

Under the New Deal attacks have been made on our civil liberties more vicious than at any period since the days immediately following the World War. Gag and loyalty bills have been rushed through our legislatures. Labor organizers have been seized, kidnapped, maltreated, killed.

The militia has been used to crush attempts of labor to organize. Lynching, race discrimination, and the development of fascist trends have continued unabated. Against these infringements of human rights the Democratic administration has kept on ominous silence.

Under the New Deal we are now spending on our Army and Navy three times as much as before the World War.

Under the capitalist Old Deal and the capitalist New Deal America has drifted increasingly toward insecurity, suppression, and war.

Insecurity is but the logical result of the workings of capitalism. For under capitalism, new and old, the many work for the owners of the machines and land. The owners will not employ the workers unless they expect to extract a profit. Labor is forced to divide up its earnings with the owning group.

With their scanty wages, the workers are able to buy only a part of the goods which they create. Goods pile up. Factories close. Workers are discharged. The country finds itself face to face with another depression.

In the past after a period of hard times we could depend upon the settlement of the West, the development of new foreign markets, and the rapid expansion of our population to revive industry. These forces can no longer be depended upon, as formerly, to keep the system going while our gross and unjust inequality of wealth, our monopoly prices, and our growing debt structure are sowing the seeds of more tragic depressions in the days ahead.

Our capitalist system is also sowing the seeds of dictatorship. As unemployment increases under capitalism the masses, to save themselves from starvation, are compelled to make even greater demands on the Government for relief and for public jobs. These demands are resisted by the propertied classes, fearful of higher taxes. Restlessness grows.

Demands for greater appropriations increase. The struggle between the House of Have and the House of Want becomes ever more intense. Big business seeks to deny the masses their constitutional rights. Fascist trends develop, trends that only a powerful and militant labor movement on the economic and political fields can successfully stay.

Militarism, likewise, under a declining capitalism, becomes an ever greater menace. As unrest increases, the masters of industry seek to use the military forces as the bulwark of reaction at home. They support higher military budgets. They look toward imperialist ventures abroad as a means of diverting attention from the unrest at home, and of gaining new markets, new investment areas, new sources of raw material.

A race begins that can have but one ending—an international war. The Japanese seizure of Manchuria and Italy's invasion of Ethiopia are but examples of the forces at work under capitalism. These adventures may well be the forerunners of another world conflict.

In socialism and in socialism alone we find the solution of our problem. Under socialism the socially necessary industries would be socially owned and democratically administered by workers, consumers, and technicians. The farmer working his own farm would be secure in his possession. The workers would no longer be forced to pay tribute to private owners. They would be able to buy back the goods they created.

Industry, finding a market for these goods, would run to capacity without periodic breakdowns. Unemployment and the waste of unplanned industry would cease. Our national income would double or treble. Every useful worker would be assured of high living standards, short hours, freedom of thought and action, and a chance to live the good life. The young would be guaranteed an opportunity for a well-rounded education. The old, the sick, the invalided would be assured the necessaries of life. Industrial autocracy and war would pass. An economy of scarcity would give way to an economy of abundance.

Such a society cannot be obtained without a mighty struggle. That struggle must be made both by workers and farmers, organized on the economic and political fields and dedicated to the creation of a cooperative commonwealth.

In their fight for power and socialism the workers and farmer must gain new strength and unity by their daily struggle against poverty and exploitation. To improve the conditions of life and labor and thereby to weld together the strength and solidarity of the masses, the Socialist Party pledges itself to fight for a number of immediate proposals in legislative halls and side by side with labor in field and factory and office.

a. We propose the adaptation of the Constitution to the needs of the times through the farmers' and workers' rights amendment, ending the usurped power of the Supreme Court to declare social legislation unconstitutional and reaffirming the right of Congress to acquire and operate industries. We also propose to change the Constitution so as to make future amendments less difficult and pledge our continued support of the child-labor amendment.

b. We propose the social ownership and democratic control of mines, railroads, the power industry, and other key industries and the recognition of public industries of the right of collective bargaining.

c. We propose an immediate appropriation by Congress of $6,-000,000,000 to continue Federal relief to the unemployed for the coming year; the continuance of W.P.A. projects at union wages; the inauguration of a public-housing program for the elimination of the nation's slums and the building of modern homes for the workers at rents they can afford to pay; a Federal system of unemployment insurance and of old-age pensions for persons 60 years of age and over, with contributions for such social-insurance systems to be raised from taxes on incomes and inheritances, as provided in the Frazier-Lundeen bill; and adequate medical care of the sick and injured as a social duty, not as a private or public charity. Such services should be financed by taxation and should be democratically administered.

d. We propose the passage of the American Youth Act to meet

the immediate educational and economic needs of young people; adequate Federal appropriations for public schools and free city colleges with a view to making possible a full education for all young people; and the abolition of the Civilian Conservation Corps, the National Youth Administration, and other governmental agencies dealing with the youth problem which threaten the wage and the living standards of organized labor.

e. We propose a drastic increase of income and inheritance taxes on the higher income levels and of excess-profits taxes and wide experimentation in land-value taxation.

f. We propose the establishment of the 30-hour week; the abolition of injunctions in labor disputes; the prohibition of company unions, company spying, and private guards and gunmen; and the prohibition of the use of police, deputy sheriffs, and militia and Federal troops in labor disputes.

g. We propose the abolition of tenant and corporation farming and the substitution of the use-and-occupancy title for family-sized farms and the conversion of plantations and corporation farms into cooperative farms. We propose that the marketing, processing, and distribution of farm products be taken over by bona fide cooperatives and other agencies to be created for this purpose. We propose that farm prices be stabilized at cost of production to the working farmer, such stabilization to be made by representatives of organized working farmers and consumers.

While these changes are taking place we urge:

(a) that immediate relief be provided for debt-laden working farmers by advancing Government credit on such terms as do not threaten the farmer with the loss of his farm.

(b) that social insurance be provided against crop failures.

h. We urge the abolition of all laws that interfere with the right of free speech, free press, free assembly, and the peaceful activities of labor in its struggle for organization and power; the enforcement of constitutional guarantees of economic, political, legal, and social equality for the Negro and all other oppressed minorities; and the enactment and enforcement of a Federal anti-lynching law.

i. Not a penny, not a man to the military arms of the Government. We reaffirm our opposition to any war engaged in by the

American Government. We propose the elimination of military training from our schools; the abandonment of imperialistic adventures of a military or economic nature abroad; the maintenance of friendly relations with Soviet Russia; and the strengthening of neutrality laws, to the end that we may ward off immediate wars while fighting for the attainment of a social order which will eliminate the chief causes of war.

j. We recognize the importance of the consumers' cooperative movement, though realizing that it alone cannot be depended upon to achieve a Socialist cooperative commonwealth. We urge the Socialist and the organized-labor movement to give their support to consumers' cooperatives to the end that it may become a valuable auxiliary to labor on the economic and political fields, and that it may help lay the foundation for a new economic order. We urge the encouragement by the Federal Government by every legitimate means of genuine consumers' cooperation.

The Socialist Party calls upon the workers, farmers, and all advocates of social justice to join with it in its struggle to widen the channels through which may be made peaceful, orderly, and democratic progress; to resist all trends toward insecurity, fascism, and war; to strengthen labor in its battles for better conditions, and for increasing power; to refuse to support the parties of capitalism, or any of their candidates, and to unite with it in its historic struggle toward a cooperative world.

VIII

American Socialism
in the Contemporary World

NORMAN THOMAS ONCE SAID THAT SOCIALISM FAILED TO MAKE substantial headway in American life and politics during the Great Depression and after for one reason: Roosevelt. The New Deal enacted with such vigor and speed in the 1930's took the thunder out of any appeal socialism might have had for most Americans. In the classic American pattern of reform rather than revolution, the Democratic party enacted into law and institutionalized a series of programs that affected almost every sector of the economy and society. Though much of the New Deal resembled the long held tenets of American socialism, it is too simple to hold that socialism influenced or frightened the older parties very much. The New Deal lacked two things basic to socialism: a deep seated urge to abolish capitalism, and planned production and distribution.

The socialist party's history since the 1930's is one of decline. Thomas polled a scant 100,000 votes in 1940. When World War II broke out in 1941, socialism was again saddled with pacifism. Party membership declined further, though war did not silence its vocal spokesmen as it had a generation earlier.

In 1948, Thomas made his last educational political campaign, polling some 140,000 votes. In 1950 the party debated the question of withdrawing from active politics, since Thomas flatly refused to run again. In 1952, Darlington Hoopes ran on the socialist ticket for president and received a tiny 20,000 votes. The party was dead politically on the state and local levels, once its most impressive field of labor. This election marked the end of serious socialist campaigning. The party, since designated the Socialist Party/Social

Democratic Federation, now relies on education rather than electioneering to attain its goals. It issues platforms though it runs no candidates, and its manifestos and declarations lack none of the force of its earlier golden age. To its credit, the party has come to grips in its writings and among its membership with complex modern problems like urbanization, disarmament, racism, and social conformity which the older parties still shun.

After 1933 many intellectuals and young people left socialism to work more actively in the New Deal atmosphere. It lost some of its appeal to intellectuals. The rise of world communism further reduced its attractiveness to most Americans, who erroneously identified it with communism. The idea that things "socialistic" are merely preludes to things "communistic" is historically unsound, especially in America. The party of Debs and Thomas had few ties and little in common with Russian communism, or with the American variety. But the socialists are not likely ever to escape entirely that kind of thinking. If the American movement has a future it is as a force for education. Its members and sympathizers, however comforting and meaningful they may find socialism, will need both patience and eloquence.

Whatever its future, American socialism merits study for its past. In its own right it was colorful, dynamic, vividly interesting in its philosophy and politics. In its attitudes toward the great issues of the twentieth century it says much, directly and indirectly, of American radicalism and of American life in general. Its influences have often been subtle and hard to define, but one feels them from reading its record.

1

"The Socialist Party Platform, 1956"

The party's platform in this year is noteworthy for its inclusive nature, its restraint combined with eloquence, and its psychological as well as practical suggestions for modern man. From Porter and Johnson, American Party Platforms, 1840-1956 *(Urbana, Illinois:*

The Socialist Party is pledged to building a new, more democratic society in the United States; a society in which human rights come before property rights; a nation which can take its place in a world federation of Cooperative Commonwealths which will eliminate war, racial antagonism, hunger, disease, poverty, and oppression.

The Socialist Party is pledged to building and to maintaining this new society by democratic means, for without freedom there can be no true socialism and without socialism there can be no enduring freedom.

Socialism is the social ownership and democratic control of the means of production. Social ownership, which includes cooperatives, is not usually government ownership. Democratic control is not administration by the central government but control by the people most directly affected and in the interest of all the people rather than for profit. The American people have already adopted many socialist measures to serve their needs when capitalism, with its profit motive, failed them.

In a big business economy the claim that "free enterprise" and liberty go hand-in-hand is arrant nonsense. The power of monopoly is a threat to the democratic process. The right of the few to rob the many is a flagrant denial of freedom. Not until the robbery is ended can we have liberty, equality and fraternity.

The Socialist Party is committed to a policy of forthright, deliberate, planned introduction of socialism. Creeping socialism when capitalism fails does not promote the welfare of the people or preserve democracy and freedom.

The Socialist Party of the United States is dedicated to building socialism in this stronghold of capitalism because, even at its greatest, capitalism fails to satisfy the finest aspirations of its people. For war it achieved great heights of productivity; for peace, it is incapable of equal performance. The development of the highest living standard in the world cannot excuse the inequality in division of wealth, which means that one family in ten receives an annual income of less than $1,000 and more than two families in ten have less than $2,000 per year. In fact, the lower half of our population receives a smaller share of the total money income of the United States now than it did early in this century.

Our program is international as well as domestic. The American people do not share fairly in the wealth they themselves create; still less have the people of the underdeveloped areas been helped to pull themselves up to a level of decency which alone can provide the stability for enduring peace. The basic purpose of socialist foreign policy is to prevent another world war. The first step is to abolish every form of colonialism, racism, and imperialism, wherever it appears, and no matter upon whose toes we tread. The second step is the encouragement of the developing democratic socialism in Asia and the movements for racial justice in Africa.

These policies will have far greater appeal to the hungry and oppressed millions of Asia, Africa, Eastern Europe, and Latin America than will military aid and defensive pacts which threaten to involve them in nuclear war. It will provide them with greater benefits than totalitarian Communism can offer, without any of its ugly evils. The democratic challenge to totalitarianism can be made successful only through rejecting imperialism and adopting democratic socialism, thus winning the minds and hearts of the downtrodden and oppressed everywhere. But most important of all we advocate these policies because they are morally right.

In this struggle, American Socialists find their allies around the world in the Socialist International and the Asian Socialist Conference and they look for the strengthening of the United Nations as a step in the development toward federal world government.

American foreign policy must be based on an imaginative campaign for universal disarmament, including the ending of the production of fission and thermonuclear weapons, under effective international supervision and control. This is absolutely essential if the living standards of the underprivileged half of the world are to be raised. As long as we spend billions for armaments there is little likelihood that large scale economic aid to underdeveloped nations will be forthcoming. The ending of thermonuclear tests is one way in which the United States could demonstrate its sincerity in seeking disarmament. Another way is by the abolition of peace-time military conscription.

The new society for which the Socialist Party strives would organize the American economy to produce for the welfare of the many at home and abroad rather than the profits of the favored few.

Capitalism fails to guarantee basic security to the people. We would establish social insurance with adequate provision for unemployment compensation, old-age pensions, and death benefits, and provide for medical care, family allotments, and sickness insurance.

Private enterprise threatens the future of the country by the waste or destruction of our irreplaceable natural resources. We would conserve these resources by the most carefully planned use under organizations like the TVA.

Private enterprise inevitably develops giant business and monopolies which threaten the economic or political welfare of the people. Socialists would step in and operate public utilities, basic industry, banks, and insurance companies either by genuine cooperatives or by publicly owned and democratically managed corporations. Private enterprise inevitably encourages the recurring collapse of individual capitalist enterprises thus threatening the livelihood of the workers involved. Sectional unemployment—whether by locality or by industry—cannot be tolerated, regardless of how high the general economic level may remain. Partial measures like adequate insurance, retraining for workers, financing movement to new work, may suffice in some situations. But where private enterprise ceases to offer opportunities for productive work, social enterprise must take over and provide them. The right of a job is a basic right which should be guaranteed to all people.

In seeking greater social controls over the American economy, Socialists would guard against the substitution of irresponsible state bureaucracy . To achieve this we propose that:

Wherever possible, the public enterprise should be at least one step removed from government control, not the patronage-run post office but the TVA is a better form.

Wherever efficient management is possible on a decentralized basis, socialists prefer this to operation on a national basis.

Wherever the people themselves can organize the needed institution, popular participation should be given preference. Cooperatives should be aided and encouraged to expand.

Wherever a public form of enterprise is set up, various categories of workers in the industry and of consumers must be represented in its control. At all times preservation of freedom of labor organization and of consumer choice is the safeguard of liberty. Social control must extend democracy and not create a new managerial hierarchy. . . .

While working towards these Socialists goals, Socialists are acutely aware of other pressing immediate problems which the American people must face in this presidential year.

The first of these is the achievement of full equality for all Americans, regardless of race, sex, creed, color, or national origin. We applaud the Supreme Court decisions that separate but equal facilities do not provide the same opportunity for all citizens in exercise of their constitutional liberties, particularly the right to vote.

We oppose any action by Congress which will surrender to the individual states the right to legislate on matters which by their nature should be under the direction of the Federal Government. This includes laws on sedition, as well as legislation affecting interstate commerce.

The second is the protection and improvement of the American standard of living. The growing threat of unemployment, both from automation and from other forces, must be met primarily by increasing workers' wages but also by expanded insurance coverage and by increasing governmental action to influence investment and production. Community needs such as schools, slum clearance, flood controls, etc., provide a wide area for useful work and stimulus to renewed productivity; we need a Point Five for America.

Taxation policies must be revised to get back to the idea of taxation in accordance with ability to pay.

We favor the establishment of government agencies or cooperatives to assist in the expansion of domestic and export consumption of farm products, to strengthen the family type farm, and to facilitate the shift from farm work to non-farm employment. But we oppose unequivocally any plan to limit the production of food or its destruction in order to keep up prices. In today's hungry world we advocate the production of more, rather than less, food.

While planning to achieve equity for the farmer, we do not forget the farm laborer or the plight of the migrant farm worker. It is essential that they be provided with steady employment, minimum wage standards, maximum hours and working conditions comparable with those of other workers and that they be provided with adequate housing and equal and identical schooling for their children.

The decline of American democracy is attested by the fact that minority parties—old or future—are being driven from the ballot by restrictive legislation; from access to the people by the incredible expense of television and new advertising techniques; and out of public favor by a manufactured conformity which stifles creative statesmanship in majority as well as minority political life.

Trade unions, too, are under attack. We continue to call for repeal of the Taft-Hartley act. So-called "right-to-work" laws passed and pending in various states, pretend to safeguard the rights of the individual to work while actually depriving him of his only real protection on the job—his union shop.

The right to work has another aspect. Where employment of persons might endanger the security of the nation, screening is a natural part of qualification for the position—and most jobs have qualifications attached. But this necessity has been distorted almost beyond recognition. Individuals must not be deprived of the right to work at non-sensitive positions for which training and experience fit them.

The right to hear and answer charges which may affect the livelihood, liberty, or citizenship of the individual must be protected by law. We ask the elimination of the Committee on Un-American Activities which has abused the Congressional right of investigation. We oppose any Congressional investigations into areas of personal belief.

We demand repeal of the Smith Act, which we protested long before its provisions were applied to the Communist Party and when that Party supported its use against other minorities. . . .

Such, in brief, is the platform of the Socialist Party. This program is based on the highest ideals of human brotherhood. It will bring peace instead of war. It will replace fear and hate with goodwill and love. Death and despair will give way to life and hope.

We urge you to join with us in a call for a democratic Socialist economy with production for use, social planning for the benefit of all, equality of opportunity, and full recognition of the dignity of every human being.

2

"Socialist Platform, 1960"

In 1960 the party ran no national candidate, but issued a very comprehensive statement of ideals and a political platform in pamphlet form. It is lengthy, and the following excerpts are designed merely to show to what extent and in what manner American socialism has come to grips with the complex problems of modern life. From Socialist Platform, 1960 *(New York: Socialist Party/Social Democratic Federation, 1960). By permission of the Socialist Party/ Social Democratic Federation.*

THE DILEMMA OF MODERN MAN

Never have Americans talked more about the importance of the private citizen; never has he felt more powerless in the face of events.

We possess the tools to build a world of peace and prosperity, and use them instead to engage in a deadly arms race. We possess the power to abolish poverty, yet unemployment continues. We possess the time to devote ourselves to great causes, but can find nothing to believe in.

From earliest schooldays to the age of retirement, on the job and at home and in our use of leisure time, when we buy and when we vote, we are subjected to a barrage of commercial, political, and social hucksterism. Our lives are shaped by public and private bureaucracies, self-perpetuating and outside our immediate control. Leaders in every field, who should be our servants, see us not as people but as *things* to be lied to, prodded, and manipulated into acquiescence. We live in a rigged society, in that the whole economy depends on the manufacture of consent, *our* consent—to planned obsolescence, to tailfins instead of schools, to cold war and the armaments race. We live frustrated lives, because we are allowed to express our yearnings only through commercially-successful channels. We live trammelled lives, because dissent is stifled. We live cheap lives, because we are taught to value ourselves cheaply.

If we are to be free, we must discover new patterns for our lives. And then we must live according to those patterns, in the midst of a hostile society, until we have created nothing less than a new social order, a society in which the commanding value is the infinite preciousness of the human spirit and of every single man, woman, and child.

For man must master society instead of being mastered by it. This is the most fundamental statement of the socialist goal. . . .

THE SOCIALIST VISION

Our goal is a new and truly democratic society in the United States, a society in which human rights come before property rights. We are pledged to building and maintaining this new society by democratic means. . . .

Socialists call for social ownership and democratic control of the commanding heights of industry, not as an end in itself, but as a step in the creation of a truly human society in which all economic and class barriers to individual freedom have been removed. . . .

We do *not* propose totalitarian nationalization as under Communism. We oppose it because in theory it is oriented toward the welfare of posterity, at the expense of the welfare and even the human dignity of the present generation; and because in practice it means that the economy is run for the benefit of the bureaucratic class that controls the state. Neither do we propose simply nationalization with political democracy; for under such a system the people participate only at election time in the decisions that control their lives. We propose rather a society of free, continuing, and democratic *participation*—through political parties in the determination of basic economic and social and political policy for the nation; through shop councils, consumer cooperatives, neighborhood associations, and all the other organs of community in the decisions of daily life; through decentralized agencies for the management of each industry by those most affected by it; through encouragement of the maximum expression of individual creativity. . . .

FOREIGN POLICY

The present conflict has often been presented as ideological. To the Western nations, it is the struggle of democracy against totalitarianism; to the Communists, it is a contest between "socialism" and "capitalism." Yet beneath these descriptions exists a more sordid reality of two rival alliances each seeking economic, social, and political power. In the Soviet Union, the military bureaucracy and, doubtless, other elements, have acquired a stake in the continuation of a cold war which brings them prestige and power. Likewise in the United States the military, the great corporations, and many scientists have acquired a vital material interest in the arms race. For this reason the economics of disarmament must be a major concern of socialist planning.

No political solution can be achieved by opposing Communist imperialism with free-enterprise capitalism. Democracy is debased when Soviet satellites are called "People's Democracies"; freedom is debased when the word "free" is applied to any despot allied to the West. . . .

The situation cries out for political, economic, and moral support by the United States of *all* struggles for self-determination, of *all* efforts of people everywhere to free themselves from exploitation. If we wish the friendship of those who seek freedom, we must cease making alliances of expediency with tyrannous regimes; we must cease our dogmatic espousal of "capitalism" which other nations cannot understand, could not use, and do not want. We must learn to support the demand of underdeveloped countries for independence, and we must support them *on their terms.* We must make their new independence meaningful by underwriting democratic paths to industrialization. . . .

A socialist foreign policy is wholly inconsistent with indefinite continuation of the Cold War and the arms race. In that race neither national security nor human freedom can be achieved. At most, balance of terror can give only a little time for precarious peace behind the so-called shield of deterrence. . . .

DISARMAMENT

[We demand] universal disarmament down to a police level for maintaining order within nations and between nations. Such disarmament may be achieved by stages; but to be genuine and enduring it must rapidly become universal and total. It must be begun by a treaty ending tests of atomic weapons above or below ground. . . . No risk is as great as a continuance of tests adding inevitably to the hazards of atomic fallout and inviting nation after nation to join the nuclear club, thereby tremendously increasing the danger of war by accident or design.

If no agreement should be reached at Geneva, the Socialist Party will call for the immediate unilateral cessation of nuclear weapons production and testing by this government. We will propose that U.N. teams be invited to establish monitoring stations on our territory for the purpose of proving to the world the reality of our action. We would then be in a sound position to call upon the Soviet Union to take similar action. Present U.S. nuclear power is such that the unilateral action we outline would not impair our security but would, on the contrary, break the present stalemate and create a new possibility—of turning the arms race into a disarmament race. . . .

STRENGTHENING THE UNITED NATIONS

The strengthening of the United Nations and the creation or strengthening of regional federations [is essential]. Such regional federations are peculiarly necessary to the healthy economy of the emerging nations of Africa. Our present imperfect U.N. has proved its value, but cannot adequately serve the great cause of peace without some revision of its charter and some provision for an international police force subject only to it, adequate to deal with brush fire wars before they kindle the great conflagration. The appeal to law instead of war must be strengthened by the repeal of the Connolly reservations under which the United States is the judge of the cases involving it that it will allow to go to the World Court. . . .

THE DOMESTIC ECONOMY

In the absence of such a [socialist] society, here and now socialists join with trade unionists and liberals in demanding immediate action:

a. For a higher minimum wage, from which farm labor must not be excluded.

b. For an integrated national campaign against poverty, with massive Federal aid to housing, community services, and education.

c. For a program of public investment as an anti-recession measure.

d. For an Area Redevelopment Bill to provide aid for distressed sections of the nation—a Point Four for our own underdeveloped regions.

e. For a national resources policy which will extend the program which proved itself in the Tennessee Valley Authority to other areas of the country, such as the Columbia River Valley and the Missouri River Valley.

f. For socialization of the oil industry on terms that give due regard to the needs and interests of a world peculiarly dependent on oil. Today this industry is a power unto itself influencing domestic and foreign policy. Socialization of the oil industry must include social ownership of the oil fields.

g. For socialization of basic means of transportation. We deplore and oppose the tendency to subsidize railroad passenger traffic while allowing private operators to reap the profits from freight traffic.

h. For overhauling our confused system of taxation, imposing withholding taxes on dividends, ending favoritism to the oil industry, regulating exemptions on expense accounts, and imposing a tax for the recovery of socially-created rental values of land. We oppose general sales taxes, which hit low-income families the hardest. . . .

SOCIAL WELFARE

. . . Unemployment compensation must be made available to all citizens who cannot find work, for as long as they remain unemployed. It should amount to two-thirds of normal income. The Federal government must supplement compensation payments (1) by creating jobs, where unemployment is general; (2) by introducing new industry into depressed areas, or relocating the unemployed where this cannot be done; (3) by retraining those displaced by technological change. . . .

Social Security should not be, as it is today, merely a palliative measure designed to supplement the savings of retired citizens. It must be extended to become a true national pension plan, designed to supply the full economic security necessary for a dignified and fruitful old age. Payments should be much higher than they are now, must be pegged to the cost-of-living index, and must be available to all persons of appropriate age regardless of their prior contributions in taxes. . . .

MEDICAL CARE

. . . We propose a National Health Service for the United States which will provide every man, woman, and child in this country with the best available medical care. We regard it as a scandal that health care in America is still run on the antiquated, nineteenth century basis of cash and carry. Nations whose resources are much less than those of America have proved that socialized medicine is the way to safeguard national health while retaining a maximum of individual freedom in the doctor-patient relationship. The American people should not be denied the benefits which the citizens of Great Britain, Scandinavia, and other countries enjoy. . . .

OTHER SOCIAL REFORMS

Our social services must be expanded and strengthened to provide for more adequate treatment and rehabilitation of the victims of alcoholism and narcotic addiction. They should be strengthened to deal more adequately with mental illness and the ravages of community and family deterioration.

It cannot be expected that our competitive and segregated society will effectively prevent juvenile delinquency. However, we urge the immediate provision of ample Federal financial aid for carefully-prepared projects for preventing and treating juvenile delinquency.

We urge the institution of a full scale program for rehabilitation of criminals as well as for eradication of the societal and environmental causes of criminal behavior. We are opposed to the punitive rather than the rehabilitative approach to criminal jurisprudence, and consequently we regard capital punishment as a grim and uncivilized vestige of the past. We pledge ourselves to work for its eradication. . . .

CIVIL RIGHTS

The immediate political fight [for civil liberties] focuses upon the attainment of a meaningful Civil Rights Act. It must include:

a. Adequate guarantees of the right of Negroes to vote, with the power of action, once a pattern of discrimination is found, vested in the Executive.

b. Legislation requiring the Federal government to initiate legal action on behalf of school integration, voting rights, or any other civil right.

c. Adoption of the principle that only integrated institutions shall qualify for Federal funds.

d. Implementation of Section 2 of the Fourteenth Amendment, depriving states of representation in Congress in proportion to the number of citizens they deprive of the right to vote on account of race, color, or previous servitude. . . .

URBAN PROBLEMS

As immediate steps to meet the problems of our cities, we advocate:

a. A Department of Urban Development, with a cabinet-rank Secretary in the Federal government.

b. National sponsorship of satellite cities to reduce urban congestion and to provide a decent environment for the rearing of children and the enjoyment of life.

c. Permanent and automatic reapportionment of all state legislatures subject to review by the courts, so as to end minority domination of state governments, and so that city governments will no longer find it necessary to bypass the state and look for aid solely to the Federal government.

d. Federal matching funds for metropolitan planning, sewer control, water-works expansion, and mass transportation.

e. Public ownership and non-profit operation of power and transportation utilities. . . .

EDUCATION

We favor Federal aid for school construction, for higher teacher salaries, and for guidance services. We favor a Federal college scholarship plan. We oppose giving Federal aid to the communities which refuse to integrate their school system as required by the May 1954 decision of the Supreme Court. We favor the extension of unionism among teachers. We oppose loyalty oaths in schools and colleges, for either teachers or students, because their only effect is to create a climate of suspicion incongruous to education in a free society. . . .

3

We end our study of American socialism's record where we began, with the question: Why be a socialist? So much has happened in the world and in America since the confident and naive days of the turn of the century that the question takes on new meaning. The following three statements are reprinted from a party pamphlet, We Have a Vision . . . A Deep Faith *(New York: Socialist Party/Social Democratic Federation, 1960). By permission of the Socialist Party/Social Democratic Federation.*

a. *A statement from Erich Fromm, noted psychologist and social philosopher:* Why join the SP/SDF? Because the SP/SDF is uniquely capable of acting as the intellectual and moral conscience of America. It is a voice that speaks of the realities of our life; it penetrates through the fog of fictions and irrelevancies now obscuring those realities.

Man is on the verge of the most crucial choice he has ever made. Will he use his skill and brain to make a world designed to encourage the fullest possible realization of his potentialities, a world of joy and creativity? Or will he make a world which will destroy him, if not with atomic bombs, then with boredom and emptiness?

Most people today believe that we can choose only between a capitalist society or a Khrushchevist managerial society. Socialists believe that there is a way out of this dilemma: the establishment of a truly democratic industrial society, centered not around things but around human beings, their hopes and dreams.

Socialism differs from other party programs in that it has a vision, an ideal for a better, more human society than the present one. Socialism not only wants to improve this or that defect of capitalism; it wants to accomplish something which does not yet exist; it aims at a goal which transcends the given empirical social reality, yet which is based on a real potentiality. Socialists have a vision, and say "this is what we want; this is what we strive for. It is not the absolute and the final—but it is a much better, more human form of life." It is the realization of the ideals of humanism which have inspired the greatest achievements of Western and Eastern culture.

Many will say that people do not want ideals, that they do not want to go beyond the frame of reference in which they live. We socialists believe that, on the contrary, people have a deep longing for something they can look for, work for, have faith in. Man's whole vitality depends on the fact that he transcends the routine part of his existence, that he strives for fulfillment of a vision that is not impossible for him to realize. If he has no chance to strive for a rational, humanistic vision, eventually, worn out and frustrated by the boredom of his life, he falls prey to the irrational and satanic visions of dictators and demagogues. It is exactly the weakness of present day capitalism that it offers no ideals, that it demands no faith, that it has no vision except more of the same.

We socialists are not ashamed to confess that we have a deep faith in man and in a vision of a new, human form of society. In urging our fellow citizens to share our vision and our attempt to realize it, we appeal to their imagination, faith, and hope. We offer them not merely a social-economic and political program, but a human program: the realization of the ideals of humanism under the conditions of an industrial society.

b. *A statement by Murray Kempton, newsman and author.* I have come to the Socialist Party (SP/SDF) because I cannot conceive of living out my life in a world without hope.

The ideal of democratic socialism has often been defeated in the world; it has never died. It has been harder to kill than any notion which moved great numbers of men at the beginning of this century. We have just concluded one of the darkest decades in human history; yet almost every light we have had toward something better has been held up in that night by a democratic socialist. Those Hungarian intellectuals who began this decade's bravest display of the human spirit thought of themselves as struggling back toward democratic socialism. If Boris Pasternak is anything, he is a democratic socialist. When Milovan Djilas went off to Tito's prison, he was asked to identify himself, and this man, without rank or trade, answered simply and proudly: "Social Democrat." And they are all men who will return because they are the guardians of man's future. Looking at them, we know that America, its life, its politics, its very voice, is governed by a dead idea. Few men worth their salt in all time have been moved long by the dream of personal private avarice; no men worth their salt are moved any longer by it today. The Voice of America is a dead echo, because the dream is dead, and the very voices are the voices of the dead played on a worn record with a broken needle left there by an engineer who went out to lunch and never came back.

I have tried living for eighteen years outside the ideal of democratic socialism. It worked as badly in my case as it has worked in the case of my country. I feel as though I have returned to the family of the human species.

c. *Statement by Dr. William C. Davidon, nuclear physicist of the Argonne National Laboratories.* Why join the SP/SDF? Because present international policies, in spite of exchanges of words and smiles, are taking us toward mass death. Our cities are being transformed into potential crematoriums; all who live in them may be turned into boiling dismembered masses within less than an hour by the decisions of a few men in a submarine, a bomber, or a missile base. Both major parties identify the indiscriminate slaughter of populations with "Defense"; neither seriously challenged the decision recently made to assist other countries to rely on nuclear weapons; neither has protested the intensified development of biological and chemical poisons and the indoctrination of the public to accept them. A few, primarily in the Democratic Party, have made mild protests; yet even Senator Humphrey was easily convinced of the necessity of providing nuclear weapons information and equipment for the rearming of West Germany and others. And beyond words, there is a lack of the tangible events that would be taking place if intentions for changing the course of present developments were seriously founded. Support of those with a mere facade of concern in a situation which calls for major change is not realism.

Why join the SP/SDF? Because people in large areas of the world are moving forward, challenging the talents and efforts of men to constructively apply their understanding and productivity. We could be a part of this frontier society, sharing in the vigor and purpose that comes from battling disease, hunger, illiteracy, from harnessing rivers, from building homes and schools. Our nation, if it were true to its heritage, would offer leadership to this changing world. Yet our society has been unable to cope with its local abundance. In a starving world, we have left idle over the past five years more than one hundred billion dollars of industrial potential. We squander hundreds of millions of dollars in yearly changes in the shapes of our cars, not to mention the ten thouand dollars that the average U.S. family has spent on the cold war. In a world as increasingly interdependent as ours the essential needs are for international solidarity, the sharing of aspirations, creativity, and labor. They cannot be met by men inculcated with lusts for draining from their society all that they can.

We cannot act imaginatively and creatively in the world today, we cannot meet the possibilities of our times, we certainly cannot resolve the international crisis that afflicts us, so long as we remain stultified by a social and economic system that rewards greed and avarice, honors oppression, ennobles waste. If we wish to lead the world to freedom, we must first free ourselves. Neither of the two old parties shows the slightest capacity for the creative thinking and action that is needed. Democratic socialism offers a way forward.

Science can assist us in making us vividly aware of what is reality and what only passes by that name. It provides us with an example of men with goals transcending their personal lives working together all over the world, building from one generation to the next. As a scientist, I have learned that objectivity and reality are not established by bisecting the range in the thoughts of others. In coping with revolutionary events, radical responses are the only realistic ones. Though others may decide how and when we die, we can choose how we live, and whether to work with others to enlarge the opportunities, the dignity, and the scope of our lives.

Postscript

A Letter from Norman Thomas

Mr. Thomas very kindly answered a letter from the Editor with a response, dated January 29, 1963, worthy of inclusion in this book since it gives an excellent statement of socialism's appeal.

. . . I became a socialist rather slowly. I was always interested in social reform and took a course in socialism in college, which was really a kind of "Why-socialism-is-mistaken" course but taught without bitterness or violent prejudice and [which was] factually reasonably accurate. Books had less to do with my becoming a socialist than life. Capitalism and its effects showed themselves pretty nearly at their worst in the districts of New York where I worked as a clergyman. It was my revulsion against those conditions, my growing respect for socialism, and in particular my respect for Socialist opposition to America's entry into World War I, which made me a Socialist. Corroboration of the Socialist position historically has come from none other than the British military authority, Maj. Gen. J. F. C. Fuller.

Socialism has meant much to me personally and I think it has meant more to America than the average American recognizes. I sometimes say truthfully that I am the most defeated man in America; that is to say, I have lost more elections. But I believe that I and the Socialist Party, in my time, in spite of frustration and defeat, have added substantially to the influence and education which Debs and the Party in his day so notably contributed to our common life.

I see no way of handling our complex interdependent economic order than by acceptance of the Socialist principle that production must be planned and organized for the use of all rather than primarily for the profit of the few. . . . At present for tactical reasons, the Party is not nominating candidates for President but trying to spread ideas. It invites help in that effort. The battle against poverty is by no means won. . . . It has scarcely been begun in the world. There is a challenge.

Sincerely yours,
Norman Thomas

The Eyewitness Accounts of American History Series

The Classics in History Series